D0018716

AMERICAN
POLITICAL
SPEECHES

EDITED WITH AN INTRODUCTION BY
TERRY GOLWAY

SERIES EDITOR
RICHARD BEEMAN

PENGUIN BOOKS

PENGUIN BOOKS

Published by the Penguin Group

Penguin Group (USA) Inc., 375 Hudson Street, New York, New York 10014, U.S.A.
Penguin Group (Canada), 90 Eglinton Avenue East, Suite 700, Toronto, Ontario,
Canada M4P 2Y3 (a division of Pearson Penguin Canada Inc.)
Penguin Books Ltd, 80 Strand, London WC2R 0RL, England
Penguin Ireland, 25 St Stephen's Green, Dublin 2, Ireland
(a division of Penguin Books Ltd)
Penguin Group (Australia), 250 Camberwell Road, Camberwell, Victoria 3124,
Australia (a division of Pearson Australia Group Pty Ltd)
Penguin Books India Pvt Ltd, 11 Community Centre,
Panchsheel Park, New Delhi - 110 017, India
Penguin Group (NZ), 67 Apollo Drive, Rosedale, Auckland 0632, New Zealand
(a division of Pearson New Zealand Ltd)
Penguin Books (South Africa) (Pty) Ltd, 24 Sturdee Avenue, Rosebank,
Johannesburg 2196, South Africa

Penguin Books Ltd, Registered Offices:
80 Strand, London WC2R 0RL, England

First published in Penguin Books 2012

1 3 5 7 9 10 8 6 4 2

LIBRARY OF CONGRESS CATALOGING-IN-PUBLICATION DATA
American political speeches / edited with an introduction by Terry Golway,
Richard Beeman.
p.   cm.—(Penguin civic classics)
ISBN 978-0-14-312195-4
1. Speeches, addresses, etc., American.   2. United States—Politics and
government—Sources.   3. Political oratory—United States.   4. Presidents—
United States—Messages.   I. Golway, Terry, 1955–   II. Beeman, Richard R.
E183.A494 2012
080.973—dc23

2012022945

Printed in the United States of America
Set in Adobe Caslon
Designed by Sabrina Bowers

CONTENTS

AMERICAN POLITICAL SPEECHES

SERIES
INTRODUCTION

W e introduce the Penguin Civic Classics series by presenting our readers with a paradox. On the one hand, there is an abundance of evidence establishing that the vast majority of Americans, whatever their political differences, have an intense love of their country, believing that it has been one of the most successful experiments in human freedom and opportunity that the world has ever seen. And Americans are similarly united in having a deep reverence for their Constitution, for their institutions of government, and for the system of free enterprise that has been such a powerful engine for our economic growth. Americans see all of these as playing a vital role in making the nation as successful as it has been.

But there is an equally large body of evidence suggesting that Americans' knowledge of their history and of the way in which their institutions have worked over the course of that history is embarrassingly meager. For example, a third of Americans believe that the Declaration of Independence was written after the end of the Civil War, and fewer than half can identify the three branches of our federal government. Nearly 40 percent of the students at fifty-five of America's elite colleges and universities could not place the Civil War in the correct half century, and fewer than half of them, when presented with the text of the Gettysburg Address, were able to identify it. Nor does it appear that our knowledge improves much as we move closer to the present. Another survey has revealed that more than half of high school seniors thought that Italy, Germany, or Japan was a U.S. ally during the Second World War, and only 14 percent of those seniors could name any relevant fact about U.S. involvement in the Korean War. As the distinguished historian David Mc-Cullough has lamented, "While the clamorous popular culture races on, the American past is slipping away, out of sight and out of mind. We are losing our story, forgetting who we are and what it's taken to come this far."

With these discouraging results in front of us, it is no wonder that there is a growing clamor for an increased emphasis on "civic education," defined by one leading authority as "the cultivation of the virtues, knowledge, and skills" necessary for carrying out one's role as a citizen. That very phrase, "civic education," sounds to many like a doctor's prescription: "You need to take your medicine! It may not be very pleasant, but it is something you need to do in order to ensure not only your own health but also the health of the body politic." It is our hope that reading these volumes in the Penguin Civic Classics series will be much more pleasant than taking medicine, for although these volumes will indeed help improve the reader's civic *knowledge*, we also hope that they will provide some civic *inspiration*—a genuine appreciation for, even an excitement about, some of the words, ideas, and actions that have shaped American society and government since the nation's founding.

The history represented in these volumes, from the founding of the American colonies in the seventeenth century to the adoption of America's Declaration of Independence to Abraham Lincoln's inspiring Gettysburg Address to Barack Obama's inaugural address as the first African American president in American history, is not merely a collection of names and dates to be memorized but, rather, a set of stories to be absorbed and enjoyed. And they are stories that have a real relevance and meaning to our lives today, whether we are debating the nature of America's immigration laws, the extent to which the federal government should be involved in decisions relating to our health care, or, getting even closer to home, whether local schools and school districts have the constitutional right to search a student's locker.

In these volumes, the reader will encounter nearly all the central themes in American history, as well as the dilemmas and conflicts that have provided much of the dynamism and excitement of that history. The central themes and ideas of American public life—democracy, equality, economic opportunity, the role of government in maintaining that delicate balance between public order and personal freedom, and the government's responsibility to protect certain individual rights—have never remained static, nor have they ever elicited uniform agreement among American citizens.

The very first item in Terry Golway's collection of important American speeches is a sermon given by Massachusetts governor John Winthrop, aboard the ship *Arbella,* as it transported the first Puritan settlers to the new colony. In that sermon, Winthrop described the Puritans' mission in Massachusetts Bay as one of creating a "city upon a hill," a model of virtue and purity for all others in the world to follow. But his vision of that society was in some important respects very much at odds with the values that guide America today. In the opening words of his sermon, Winthrop reminded his fellow colonists that "GOD ALMIGHTY in His most holy and wise providence, hath so disposed of the condition of mankind, as in all times some must be rich, some poor, some high and eminent in power and dignity; others mean and in submission." Hardly a prescription for the democratic society that we claim to be today.

Fast-forward 136 years to the promise contained in Thomas Jefferson's Declaration of Independence that "all men are created equal"—a view of society *very* different from that articulated by Winthrop. Jefferson's city upon a hill was to be a nation dedicated to equality and the pursuit of happiness, not to a divinely ordained, inegalitarian social hierarchy. But, of course, in a world in which Africans were enslaved, women were considered legally subordinate to men, and, indeed, many free white males were denied the right to vote because they did not own the requisite amount of property, Jefferson's promise of equality fell far short of an accurate description of the reality of American society in 1776. Still, words have power, and Abraham Lincoln, for one, knew the power of those words. As is amply displayed in Allen Guelzo's volume containing many of Lincoln's principal speeches, time and time again Lincoln invoked Jefferson's preamble as a pledge that Americans of his age were honor-bound to fulfill, describing the preamble as "the electric cord in that Declaration that links the hearts of patriotic and liberty-loving men together, that will link those patriotic hearts as long as the love of freedom exists in the minds of men throughout the world."

Alas, Americans would fight a horrific, bloody civil war in which more than 600,000 people, slave and free, lost their lives before the nation was able to take the steps necessary to forge the link to which Lincoln had referred. Beginning in December 1865, with the adoption of the Thirteenth Amendment, eliminating the institution of slavery; continuing with the adoption of the Fourteenth Amendment (July 1868), with its guarantee of "equal protection under the laws"; and culminating with the adoption of the Fifteenth Amendment (February 1870), asserting that the right to vote could not "be abridged . . . on account of race, color, or previous condition of servitude," those ideas of democracy and equality began to be incorporated into our constitutional system. But although those three amendments represented an important step forward, America's struggle to live up to the promise of the preamble was far from over. It took until 1920 for the nation to adopt the Nineteenth Amendment, giving women the right to vote, and in spite of the guarantees of the Fourteenth and Fifteenth Amendments, the civil rights of African Americans, including the right to vote, continued to be undermined by the actions of individual state governments well into the twentieth century. When Lyndon Johnson, only the second (after Woodrow Wilson) Southern-born president since the Civil War, signed into law the Voting Rights Act of

1965, he too quoted the preamble to the Declaration of Independence and ended his speech with a phrase from the anthem of the civil rights movement of the 1950s and 1960s: "We Shall Overcome." And when the first African American president, Barack Obama, delivered his inauguration speech on a cold day in January 2009, he began by paraphrasing the words of Thomas Jefferson's preamble, urging Americans "to carry forward that precious gift, that noble idea, passed on from generation to generation: the God-given promise that all are equal, all are free, and all deserve a chance to pursue their full measure of happiness." Even in 2009 those words were, like Jefferson's, expressions of hope, not descriptions of reality. But they have proved powerful indeed, and they continue to be a dynamic force in shaping the American future just as they have the American past.

Another important theme that emerges from these volumes of Civic Classics involves the age-old debate on how and where to strike the best balance between public order and personal liberty. For most of human history, those who held government power—kings or emperors or czars—usually dealt with that issue by ruthlessly imposing their own definition of what was good for the masses of people whom they governed. When Thomas Paine published his earth-shaking pamphlet *Common Sense* in January 1776, his primary purpose was to persuade the American colonists to throw off British rule, but one of the key elements in his argument was the notion that while every society needs some form of government in order to provide security and protect the freedom of its citizens, the best and freest societies are those in which government is least intrusive. In Paine's words: "Society in every state is a blessing, but government even in its best state is but a necessary evil; in its worst state an intolerable one." Paine's words struck a chord with his American readers, who were already suspicious of the overly powerful, distant government of Great Britain, and the Declaration of Independence, approved seven months later, reinforced that same theme. The distrust of concentrations of government power—the notion that government, while necessary, must be restrained—is deeply rooted in America's revolutionary past and, of course, is very much alive today, as we can observe by the vitality of political movements such as the Tea Party.

As powerful as Paine's and Jefferson's indictments of excessive British power may have been, they did not provide the answer to the question of how the independent American nation could create a government that would strike an ideal balance between order and liberty. The men who gathered in Philadelphia in the summer of 1787 to frame a new constitution for their still-fragile independent nation took a giant step forward in providing an answer when they created a governmental system based on the division of power between the individual states and the central government—the system that we now call federalism—and by further dividing power among the three branches of the federal government in a system that we characterize as one of "checks and balances."

But, as in so many other important ideas in American history, those involving federalism and checks and balances were subject to many different interpretations. Alexander Hamilton, James Madison, and John Jay, in the eighty-five essays comprising *The Federalist Papers*, attempted to address some of the concerns that Americans had about the excessive power of the proposed new federal government and, in the process, provided Americans with enduring insights about government and politics—insights that are still cited by Supreme Court justices in their judicial opinions today. But Hamilton and Madison, the two principal authors of *The Federalist Papers*, began to disagree about the relationship of the new federal government to the individual states and to the people at large almost from the moment the government commenced operation. The debate over the way the words of the Constitution should be interpreted, with Madison and Jefferson taking a "strict construction" position, and Hamilton, George Washington, and others arguing for a broader interpretation of the Constitution, has stayed with us until the present day. As readers of Jay Feinman's collection of landmark Supreme Court cases will discover, the Court has spent a significant portion of its time over the years, beginning with Chief Justice John Marshall's majority opinion in *McCulloch v. Maryland* (1819), wrestling with the extent of and limits on federal government power. Nor has that conflict been confined to judicial or intellectual arguments. In the years leading up to the Civil War, Northern and Southern politicians fought ferocious battles over the question of what authority the federal government had to legislate with respect to the expansion of slavery into new territories; once again, the ever-eloquent Abraham Lincoln weighed in on those issues, as is amply illustrated in Allen Guelzo's selection of Lincoln speeches. In the end, of course, it was not words that settled the constitutional argument between North and South but the force of arms. The Civil War was, in some senses, America's greatest civic failure, for knowledge and reason alone were not sufficient to settle the conflict between North and South. But however terrible the toll, it did resolve the paradox at the nation's core—the existence of the institution of slavery in a nation that claimed to be devoted to liberty.

Mercifully, the Civil War was the last occasion in which our differences of opinion over governmental power have resulted in warfare, but the war of words has never ceased. Whether debating issues relating to economic regulation or immigration, or providing and regulating health care, Americans—Republicans and Democrats, Tea Party members and Occupy Wall Street activists—continue to differ, sometimes passionately, on the way our Constitution should be interpreted.

Americans, perhaps more than any other people in the world, have been ardently committed to defending their "rights." Indeed, when most Americans today think of their Constitution, they think not so much about those enumerated powers such as the levying of taxes, the regulating of commerce, or the coining of money that are contained in the main body of the Constitution, but, rather, they think of the Bill of Rights. In fact, one of the few mistakes made by the framers of the Constitution in 1787 was their failure even to include a Bill of Rights in their final draft of the Constitution, a mistake that was, fortunately, remedied by the First Federal Congress in 1789. The rights articulated in our first ten amendments, including freedom of speech, the "free exercise of religion," freedom of the press, and freedom from unlawful search and seizure, have not only provided the foundation for the freedoms that we so value today but have also prompted some of our most vigorously debated controversies. Readers of Jay Feinman's volume on some of the most important Supreme Court decisions in our history will discover that, in general, the Court's definition of the rights guaranteed in those amendments has tended to widen over the course of our history. But there remain limits on the Bill of Rights protections enjoyed by Americans. For example, the right of free speech has not extended to public protests in which the threat of violence is imminent, and in an era of GPS tracking devices and CCTV cameras, Americans are confronted with new challenges in defining what constitutes an unlawful search and seizure.

The constitutional protection of individual rights has not been confined to those items specifically listed in the Bill of Rights. The Ninth Amendment, which says that the "enumeration in the Constitution, of certain rights, shall not be construed to deny or disparage others retained by the people," has been interpreted to include the right of privacy, including the right of a woman to have some control over her health and reproductive decisions. The most well known of the Supreme Court decisions relating to the right of a woman to terminate a pregnancy, *Roe v. Wade* (1973), far from settling that difficult question, has been followed by a series of subsequent Supreme Court decisions seeking to further refine and, in many cases, limit the right to obtain an abortion. The Court's decisions in these areas, far from being legal abstractions of interest only to a few history or civics teachers, have had an impact, and will continue to have an impact, on the lives of millions of women.

This series of Penguin Civic Classics is based on the belief that acquiring knowledge of America's history and of our rights and responsibilities as citizens is not merely an abstract, academic exercise. *It really matters.* It can make an actual difference in each and every one of our lives. And never more so than in the extraordinarily complicated, tumultuous, twenty-first-century world in which we live—a time of rapid, sometimes confounding, change. David McCullough has spoken of the way in which our knowledge of history and of the way in which our institutions of government operate can give us a "sense of navigation, a sense of what we've been through in times past and who we are." It can also *empower* us. If we are familiar with the way in which people in the past have confronted their problems, and if we have a decent understanding of how to make the best use of America's institutions to deal with the problems confronting us in the present, we have a much better chance of being able to control our own destinies. Our opinions of the "correct" way to proceed may not always prevail, but we will at least be participants, not passive bystanders, in the ongoing drama that is the history of the United States. And, perhaps most important of all, it is often personally more rewarding, more fun, to be a participant rather than to be a bystander.

RICHARD BEEMAN

INTRODUCTION

To understand the significance of political speeches in American history, it is important to remember that the United States is an expression of ideas, ideas that are built into centuries-old narratives which challenged the Old World's political boundaries of blood lines, class divisions, language, and creed. American civic language speaks of fidelity to principles of democracy and equality—however imperfectly applied—rather than loyalty to tribe, to aristocracy, to denomination, or even to the land itself. There is no motherland or fatherland in American rhetoric; no successful political leader in the twenty-first century can mobilize citizens with appeals to ancient political grievances or cultural memories. Americans must be moved and inspired with the power of ideas.

Ideas, of course, are best expressed in words. Americans revere their founding documents—the Declaration of Independence and the Constitution—because the Founders articulated the ideas and ideals which have remained at the core of the American experience. But the nation's self-image, aspirations, expectations, and, yes, frustrations, also are enshrined in spoken words, the words of political and civic leaders seeking to inspire, to probe, to critique, and to interpret the American experience for new and future generations. Nearly all great American oratory advances, explains, or adds context to the simple yet radical ideas that are at the heart of the American experiment—the aspiration to equality and justice, the mission to create a more perfect union, the assertion that government derives its power from the people.

The best speeches are more than words. They are the transmitters of stories which nations and people tell about themselves. And memorable political speeches are not just about the thrust and parry of partisan politics. Great political speeches transcend time, place, and issues to speak to the values, assumptions, and conventions of the American experience. American political oratory has inspired revolutions of all sorts, from the armed conflict which led to independence in the eighteenth century to the social uprising of the civil rights movement in the 1960s. Political leaders, self-appointed and elected, forgotten and famous, have used the spoken word to summon the nation's better angels, to uphold its ideals, defy its assumptions, proclaim its righteousness, and condemn its inequities. Great political speeches have electrified nominating conventions, shocked polite audiences, defended unpopular causes, proclaimed uncomfortable truths, and enunciated American values. They have been delivered in front of audiences numbering in the hundreds, and in the millions. One, in fact, was delivered to nobody—George Washington's famous farewell address in 1796 actually was not spoken at all, as is commonly thought, but was circulated in print as the nation's first president prepared to relinquish office after two terms. It was not, then, a true speech, but its importance as a foundational document in American political history is such that it demanded inclusion in this compilation.

Most political speeches are easily, and often rightly, characterized as tedious exercises in vanity on the part of the speaker and incredulity on the part of listeners. Political leaders, from the most humble town official to the President of the United States, deliver hundreds of speeches in a single year. Rare is the one that will be remembered within minutes of its conclusion. But every so often, the moment, the speaker, and the words come together to produce a speech which transcends time and place, which speaks to those principles and ideas which define the American experiment in self-government.

Many of these speeches are famous, and justifiably so. They have been recorded and preserved, and so have been transformed from spoken word to essential text. Schoolchildren born in the early years of the twenty-first century still memorize the nineteenth-century phrases of Abraham Lincoln. Old footage and sound archives ensure that generations unborn will continue to hear Franklin Roosevelt's reassuring voice in the midst of the Great Depression, or glimpse the confidence of John Kennedy as he declared that the nation would "pay any price" in defense of liberty. Citizens of the twenty-first century, and beyond, no doubt will continue to draw inspiration from Martin Luther King's dream, from the ebullient optimism of Ronald Reagan, from the passionate dissent of Frederick Douglass, and from the understated eloquence of Barbara Jordan.

We remember these orators and their speeches not

only because of the power of their words, but, in truth, because of the power of their station. As leaders, civic elites, and public figures, their words commanded attention and, just as important, transcription, thus ensuring their preservation. But surely there have been other speakers, other words, and other moments in American political history that have not been written into the record. There have been, without question, great orations in obscure places, remembered with wonder and awe by those who heard them, but recorded by no one. That is history's loss. This collection, then, must focus on speeches that, in one way or another, were preserved and transcribed, and which were delivered by noted civic leaders—although the speakers were not always holders of elective office. The former slave Frederick Douglass and the feminist crusader Carrie Chapman Catt were leaders of no political party or partisan faction, but their words were intensely political, designed as they were to shape, question, and critique the administration of justice and division of power in the United States.

Thanks to advances in print journalism in the nineteenth century, in broadcast media in the twentieth, and in digital technology in the twenty-first, we know how most of the speeches in this volume were received—what sentiments gathered the most attention, what phrases captured the public's imagination. A report in the *New York Times* on November 20, 1863, noted that President Abraham Lincoln's short speech at the dedication of a new military cemetery in Gettysburg, Pennsylvania, was interrupted by applause five times (no small achievement for a speech that took no more than a couple of minutes to deliver), and that his listeners erupted in "long, continued applause" when the President finished. Critics, of course, were somewhat less impressed—a *Times* reporter the following day referred to the President's "business-like" remarks, in contrast to the "splendid" oration of the main speaker, Edward Everett, whose speech of nearly two hours is now forgotten. Great political speeches are those which stand the test of time. Lincoln's modest address at Gettysburg did; Everett's did not.

We know less about the older speeches in this collection. For example, Patrick Henry's famous demand for liberty or death in 1775 was delivered without notes and was not transcribed. Henry's first biographer, William Wirt, reconstructed the speech in 1816 based on the account of an eyewitness. Does Wirt's version faithfully record Henry's precise words? It is impossible to know, although it is clear that Henry said something electrifying. A colleague noted that as Henry spoke, "Men leaned forward in their seats . . . their faces pale and their eyes glaring like the speaker's. . . . When he sat down, I felt sick with excitement." Even if we do not know Henry's precise words, we do know their impact. After he sat down, the colony's elected leaders approved a resolution calling for the creation of an armed force to defend Virginia's liberties.

Thomas Jefferson, in contrast with his fellow Virginian's confidently extemporaneous style, carefully prepared his Inaugural Address in 1801 as he assumed the presidency after a bitter contest with his fellow Founding Father, John Adams. But relatively few people witnessed Jefferson's speech, for inaugurations were simple affairs in the republic's infancy—the new President, in fact, simply walked to the ceremony from a nearby boardinghouse. So Jefferson's description of the United States as "the world's best hope," and his assertion that "we are all Republicans; we are all Federalists" fell on few ears. But the speech's grace notes and vision became part of the American canon despite the small audience because they expressed an exceptional vision of the new nation's mission, and because, after a historic, nonviolent transfer of power from Adams's Federalists to Jefferson's Republicans (today's Democrats), the new President chose to remind his countrymen of their shared identity and sense of mission, rather than dwell on their partisan differences.

That exceptional identity, that sense of mission, was articulated in a speech given aboard an immigrant ship, the *Arbella*, in 1630, when a lawyer named John Winthrop addressed his fellow Puritans who so loathed the old order in their native England that they chose to cross the Atlantic Ocean to establish new, more righteous lives on a continent about which they knew precious little. Winthrop delivered a short speech filled with biblical allusions which his pious fellow passengers surely would have understood. Building on a New Testament verse which proclaimed that a "city that is set on a hill cannot be hid," Winthrop announced that his fellow travelers must create a "city upon a hill," an example of righteousness that the Old World would look upon with wonder. "The eyes of the people shall be upon us," Winthrop said. Those phrases became the rock on which the notion of American exceptionalism was built. Presidents Kennedy and Reagan both mobilized the imagery of a city upon a hill in their speeches, and the words themselves are literally written in stone in one of the nation's most-revered public spaces, Boston Common.

John Winthrop was not a politician in the modern sense, and he certainly was not a democrat. He brought with him across the Atlantic a firm belief in his own righteousness and a finely tuned contempt for those who dared to differ. Nevertheless, his speech aboard the *Arbella* is the founding text in American political rhetoric, for its language of exceptionalism informed the identity and mission of the nation that would emerge from thirteen small colonies in 1776. More to the point, Winthrop's overtly religious exhortations provided a template for American political rhetoric in the centuries that followed his speech. As this collection shows, it is a rare piece of American political oratory even today that does not contain biblical imagery, an appeal to the Almighty, or the suggestion that the nation's role in world affairs has a special dispensation from on high. "The Lord will be our God and delight to dwell among us, as his own people, and will command a blessing upon us in all our ways," Winthrop told his fellow passengers shortly before they landed in a new and, they hoped, better England, an England they created in their imagination during their perilous journey across the Atlantic.

Political leaders in the centuries that followed the founding of the Massachusetts Bay Colony have often echoed Winthrop's confidence of a shared mission between the New World and the eternal heavens. "There is a just God who presides over the destinies of nations, and who will raise up friends to fight our battles for us," Patrick Henry said during the course of his "liberty or death" speech in 1775. Nearly two centuries later, as he concluded one of the most poetic and inspiring Inaugural Addresses in the nation's history, John F. Kennedy reminded his listeners that "here on earth, God's work must truly be our own."

Many of the speeches in this collection link the nation's mission and identity to an approving creator. "God will not favor everything that we do," Lyndon Johnson said in 1965 as he introduced a new voting rights act aimed at purging the nation's polls of racial discrimination. "But I cannot help believing that He truly understands and that He really favors the undertaking that we begin here tonight."

Other speeches may not invoke God's name but are redolent in language and themes taken from religious narratives. Indeed, one of the most famous speeches in this nation's political history ended with an image from the New Testament: William Jennings Bryan's defiant promise in 1896 that "you shall not press down upon the brow of labor this crown of thorns. You shall not crucify mankind upon a cross of gold." Bryan, a fundamentalist Christian from the Midwest, used powerful Christian imagery to give voice to the economic discontents of the late nineteenth century. More than three decades later, Franklin Delano Roosevelt, a mainstream Protestant from the Northeast, summoned biblical language to articulate the nation's anger during another, deeper economic crisis. "The money changers have fled from their high seats in the temple of civilization," Roosevelt said as he addressed a stricken, fearful nation for the first time as President in 1933.

"We love this country. We love this government. It is a religion, I say." So said Huey Long, a U.S. Senator from Louisiana who defied his fellow Democrat, Roosevelt, with a radical plan to resolve the nation's economic problems during the Great Depression. Long outlined his plan, which he called "Share Our Wealth," in a nationwide radio speech which required him to pause several times to identify himself to the millions who could hear, but not see, him—a new dilemma for the nation's political orators, at least those not named Franklin D. Roosevelt.

Of course, not all the speeches in this collection can trace their rhetorical roots to John Winthrop's piety and evangelical vision. Some, indeed, called into question comfortable assumptions or challenged accepted wisdom. The magnificent righteousness of the onetime slave Frederick Douglass in a July 4 speech in 1852 was a powerful reminder that the nation's commitment to liberty and freedom did not apply to him and to millions of others held in bondage. U.S. Senator Robert La Follette insisted that no democracy could shut down dissent and unpopular opinions even in a time of war. Senator Margaret Chase Smith publicly denounced colleagues—her target was fellow Republican Senator Joseph McCarthy—who chose slander over argument, defamation over facts, during the tumultuous Red Scare of the early 1950s. And Ronald Reagan argued that government played too large a role in the nation's economic life as he took office in 1981.

Each of the speeches in this collection illuminates a moment, a turn of phrase, a policy pronouncement, a defiant critique, an assertion of exceptionalism, that transcends time and setting. Each sheds light on American identity, American politics, and American policy.

Each is more than words.

TERRY GOLWAY

A NOTE
ON THE TEXT

All of the following speeches are selected excerpts with the exceptions of Abraham Lincoln's Gettysburg Address, Franklin D. Roosevelt's request for a declaration of war after Pearl Harbor, John F. Kennedy's speech at the Berlin Wall, and Martin Luther King, Jr.'s "I Have a Dream" speech in Washington, D.C. Not all excerpts begin with the original speech's opening phrases.

Chapter 1
"CITY UPON A HILL"

JOHN WINTHROP'S SPEECH ABOARD
THE *ARBELLA*, 1630

☛ John Winthrop and his fellow Puritans traveled across the Atlantic Ocean in spring 1630, convinced that the English monarchy and society were irredeemable. They sought to create a more pious community in the New World. Winthrop's speech aboard the *Arbella* was intended to give a larger purpose to their hazardous journey. He achieved much more: In describing the Puritans' venture as a "city upon a hill," he set the groundwork for America's self-image as an exceptional nation-state.

When God gives a special commission, He looks to have it strictly observed in every article. . . . Thus stands the cause between God and us. We are entered into covenant with Him for this work. We have taken out a commission. The Lord hath given us leave to draw our own articles. We have professed to enterprise these and those accounts, upon these and those ends. We have hereupon besought him of favor and blessing. Now if the Lord shall please to hear us, and bring us in peace to the place we desire, then hath He ratified this covenant and sealed our commission, and will expect a strict performance of the articles contained in it; but if we shall neglect the observation of these articles which are the ends we have propounded, and, dissembling with our God, shall fail to embrace this present world and prosecute our carnal intentions, seeking great things for ourselves and our posterity, the Lord will surely break out in wrath against us, and be revenged of such a people, and make us know the price of the breach of such a covenant.

Now the only way to avoid this shipwreck, and to provide for our posterity, is to follow the counsel of Micah, to do justly, to love mercy, to walk humbly with our God. For this end, we must be knit together, in this work, as one man. We must entertain each other in brotherly affection. We must be willing to abridge ourselves of our superfluities, for the supply of others' necessities. We must uphold a familiar commerce together in all meekness, gentleness, patience and liberality. We must delight in each other; make others' conditions our own; rejoice together, mourn together, labor and suffer together, always having before our eyes our commission and community in the work, as members of the same body. So shall we keep the unity of the spirit in the bond of peace. The Lord will be our God, and delight to dwell among us, as His own people. . . .

For we must consider that we shall be as a city upon a hill. The eyes of all people are upon us. So that if we shall deal falsely with our God in this work we have undertaken, and so cause Him to withdraw His present help from us, we shall be made a story and a by-word through the world. We shall open the mouths of enemies to speak evil of the ways of God, and all professors for God's sake. We shall shame the faces of many of God's worthy servants, and cause their prayers to be turned into curses upon us till we be consumed out of the good land whither we are going.

And to shut this discourse with that exhortation of Moses, that faithful servant of the Lord, in his last farewell to Israel. . . . "Beloved, there is now set before us life and death, good and evil," in that we are commanded this day to love the Lord our God, and to love one another, to walk in His ways and to keep His Commandments and His ordinance and His laws, and the articles of our covenant with Him, that we may live and be multiplied, and that the Lord our God may bless us in the land whither we go to possess it. But if our hearts shall turn away, so that we will not obey, but shall be seduced, and worship other gods, our pleasure and profits, and serve them; it is propounded unto us this day, we shall surely perish out of the good land whither we pass over this vast sea to possess it.

Therefore let us choose life,
that we and our seed may live,
by obeying His voice and cleaving to Him,
for He is our life and our prosperity.

Chapter 2

"GIVE ME LIBERTY, OR GIVE ME DEATH"

**PATRICK HENRY AT
ST. JOHN'S CHURCH, RICHMOND,
VIRGINIA, MARCH 23, 1775**

When Patrick Henry rose to speak on an early spring day in 1775, relations between London and thirteen British colonies in America were tense but not yet irretrievably broken. Hundreds of miles to the north, the city of Boston was chafing under military rule imposed after the famous Boston Tea Party. Boston was a long way from Virginia; many of Patrick Henry's peers among Virginia's leaders held out hope that a peaceful settlement with London remained possible. Henry begged to differ. He introduced resolutions calling on the colony to prepare to defend itself, and then sought to win his colleagues' support with this passionate address. (Note that in this speech, Henry directed his comments to the President of the House of Burgesses.)

Mr. President, it is natural to man to indulge in the illusions of hope. We are apt to shut our eyes against a painful truth, and listen to the song of that siren till she transforms us into beasts. Is this the part of wise men, engaged in a great and arduous struggle for liberty? Are we disposed to be of the number of those who, having eyes, see not, and, having ears, hear not, the things which so nearly concern their temporal salvation? For my part, whatever anguish of spirit it may cost, I am willing to know the whole truth; to know the worst, and to provide for it.

I have but one lamp by which my feet are guided; and that is the lamp of experience. I know of no way of judging of the future but by the past. And judging by the past, I wish to know what there has been in the conduct of the British ministry for the last ten years, to justify those hopes with which gentlemen have been pleased to solace themselves, and the House? Is it that insidious smile with which our petition has been lately received? Trust it not, sir; it will prove a snare to your feet. Suffer not yourselves to be betrayed with a kiss. Ask yourselves how this gracious reception of our petition comports with these war-like preparations which cover our waters and darken our land. Are fleets and armies necessary to a work of love and reconciliation? Have we shown ourselves so unwilling to be reconciled, that force must be called in to win back our love? Let us not deceive ourselves, sir. These are the implements of war and subjugation; the last arguments to which kings resort. I ask, gentlemen, sir, what means this martial array, if its purpose be not to force us to submission? Can gentlemen assign any other possible motive for it? Has Great Britain any enemy, in this quarter of the world, to call for all this accumulation of navies and armies? No, sir, she has none. They are meant for us; they can be meant for no other. They are sent over to bind and rivet upon us those chains which the British ministry have been so long forging. And what have we to oppose to them? Shall we try argument? Sir, we have been trying that for the last ten years. Have we anything new to offer upon the subject? Nothing. We have held the subject up in every light of which it is capable; but it has been all in vain. Shall we resort to entreaty and humble supplication? What terms shall we find which have not been already exhausted?

Let us not, I beseech you, sir, deceive ourselves. Sir, we have done everything that could be done, to avert the storm which is now coming on. We have petitioned; we have remonstrated; we have supplicated; we have prostrated ourselves before the throne, and have implored its interposition to arrest the tyrannical hands of the ministry and Parliament. Our petitions have been slighted; our remonstrances have produced additional violence and insult; our supplications have been disregarded; and we have been spurned, with contempt, from the foot of the throne. In vain, after these things, may we indulge the fond hope of peace and reconciliation. There is no longer any room for hope. If we wish to be free, if we mean to preserve inviolate those inestimable privileges for which we have been so long contending, if we mean not basely to abandon the noble struggle in which we have been so long engaged, and which we have pledged ourselves never to abandon until the glorious object of our contest shall be obtained, we must fight! I repeat it, sir, we must fight! An appeal to arms and to the God of Hosts is all that is left us!

They tell us, sir, that we are weak; unable to cope with so formidable an adversary. But when shall we be stronger? Will it be the next week, or the next year? Will it be when we are totally disarmed, and when a British guard shall be stationed in every house? Shall we gather strength by irresolution and inaction? Shall we acquire the means of effectual resistance, by lying supinely on our backs, and hugging the delusive phantom of hope, until our enemies shall have bound us hand and foot? Sir, we are not weak if we make a proper use of those means which the God of nature hath placed in our power. Three millions of people, armed in the holy cause of liberty, and in such a country as that which we possess, are invincible by any force which our enemy can send against us. Besides, sir, we shall not fight our battles alone. There is a just God who presides over the destinies of nations; and who will raise up friends to fight our battles for us. The battle, sir, is not to the strong alone; it is to the vigilant, the active, the brave. Besides, sir, we have no election. If we were base enough to desire it, it is now too late to retire from the contest. There is no retreat but in submission and slavery! Our chains are forged! Their clanking may be heard on the plains of Boston! The war is inevitable and let it come! I repeat it, sir, let it come.

It is in vain, sir, to extenuate the matter. Gentlemen may cry, Peace, Peace but there is no peace. The war is actually begun! The next gale that sweeps from the north will bring to our ears the clash of resounding arms! Our brethren are already in the field! Why stand we here idle? What is it that gentlemen wish? What would they have? Is life so dear, or peace so sweet, as to be purchased at the price of chains and slavery? Forbid it, Almighty God! I know not what course others may take; but as for me, give me liberty or give me death!

Chapter 3

"STEER CLEAR OF PERMANENT ALLIANCES"

GEORGE WASHINGTON'S FAREWELL ADDRESS, SEPTEMBER 19, 1796

George Washington was a less-than-stellar orator despite his imposing physical presence. As a result, his final words to the American people were not spoken. They were written, after long conversations with Alexander Hamilton and James Madison, and published in a Philadelphia-based newspaper called the *American Daily Advertiser*. Although not delivered verbally, Washington's farewell address is such an essential text that it demands inclusion in this collection as if it were a speech. In it, Washington famously warns the nation against "permanent alliances." But he also used the occasion, in his opening words, to inform his fellow citizens that he would not be a candidate for a third term in office, thus setting the two-term precedent that lasted until Franklin Roosevelt won a third term in 1940.

The period for a new election of a citizen to administer the executive government of the United States being not far distant, and the time actually arrived when your thoughts must be employed in designating the person who is to be clothed with that important trust, it appears to me proper, especially as it may conduce to a more distinct expression of the public voice, that I should now apprise you of the resolution I have formed, to decline being considered among the number of those out of whom a choice is to be made. . . .

Here, perhaps, I ought to stop. But a solicitude for your welfare, which cannot end but with my life, and the apprehension of danger, natural to that solicitude, urge me, on an occasion like the present, to offer to your solemn contemplation, and to recommend to your frequent review, some sentiments which are the result of much reflection, of no inconsiderable observation, and which appear to me all-important to the permanency of your felicity as a people. These will be offered to you with the more freedom, as you can only see in them the disinterested warnings of a parting friend, who can possibly have no personal motive to bias his counsel. . . .

Against the insidious wiles of foreign influence (I conjure you to believe me, fellow-citizens) the jealousy of a free people ought to be constantly awake, since history and experience prove that foreign influence is one of the most baneful foes of republican government. But that jealousy to be useful must be impartial; else it becomes the instrument of the very influence to be avoided, instead of a defense against it. Excessive partiality for one foreign nation and excessive dislike of another cause those whom they actuate to see danger only on one side, and serve to veil and even second the arts of influence on the other. Real patriots who may resist the intrigues of the favorite are liable to become suspected and odious, while its tools and dupes usurp the applause and confidence of the people, to surrender their interests.

The great rule of conduct for us in regard to foreign nations is in extending our commercial relations, to have with them as little political connection as possible. So far as we have already formed engagements, let them be fulfilled with perfect good faith. Here let us stop. Europe has a set of primary interests which to us have none; or a very remote relation. Hence she must be engaged in frequent controversies, the causes of which are essentially foreign to our concerns. Hence, therefore, it must be unwise in us to implicate ourselves by artificial ties in the ordinary vicissitudes of her politics, or the ordinary combinations and collisions of her friendships or enmities.

Our detached and distant situation invites and enables us to pursue a different course. If we remain one people under an efficient government, the period is not far off when we may defy material injury from external annoyance; when we may take such an attitude as will cause the neutrality we may at any time resolve upon to be scrupulously respected; when belligerent nations, under the impossibility of making acquisitions upon us, will not lightly hazard the giving us provocation; when we may choose peace or war, as our interest, guided by justice, shall counsel.

Why forego the advantages of so peculiar a situation? Why quit our own to stand upon foreign ground? Why, by interweaving our destiny with that of any part of Europe, entangle our peace and prosperity in the toils of European ambition, rivalship, interest, humor, or caprice?

It is our true policy to steer clear of permanent alliances with any portion of the foreign world; so far, I mean, as we are now at liberty to do it; for let me not be understood as capable of patronizing infidelity to existing engagements. I hold the maxim no less applicable to public than to private affairs, that honesty is always the best policy. I repeat it, therefore, let those engagements be observed in their genuine sense. But, in my opinion, it is unnecessary and would be unwise to extend them. . . .

In offering to you, my countrymen, these counsels of an old and affectionate friend, I dare not hope they will make the strong and lasting impression I could wish; that they will control the usual current of the passions, or prevent our nation from running the course which has hitherto marked the destiny of nations. But, if I may even flatter myself that they may be productive of some partial benefit, some occasional good; that they may now and then recur to moderate the fury of party spirit, to warn against the mischiefs of foreign intrigue, to guard against the impostures of pretended patriotism; this hope will be a full recompense for the solicitude for your welfare, by which they have been dictated. . . .

Chapter 4

"WE ARE ALL REPUBLICANS; WE ARE ALL FEDERALISTS."

THOMAS JEFFERSON'S FIRST INAUGURAL ADDRESS, MARCH 4, 1801

☞ The election of 1800 was among the nastiest in American history—even when compared with the hyperpartisan rhetoric of the early twenty-first century. The incumbent president, John Adams, was accused of being pro-British—quite an accusation to make against a Founding Father. The challenger, Thomas Jefferson, was said to have fathered a child with one of his slaves—an accusation which most historians now accept to be true. Jefferson defeated Adams, leading to the transfer of power from one party to another—a first in American political history. In his Inaugural Address, Jefferson sought to unify the nation after the bitter election campaign.

During the contest of opinion through which we have passed, the animation of discussion and of exertions has sometimes worn an aspect which might impose on strangers unused to think freely and to speak and to write what they think; but this being now decided by the voice of the nation, announced according to the rules of the constitution, all will, of course, arrange themselves under the will of the law, and unite in common efforts for the common good. All, too, will bear in mind this sacred principle, that though the will of the majority is in all cases to prevail, that will, to be rightful, must be reasonable; that the minority possess their equal rights, which equal laws must protect, and to violate which would be oppression.

Let us, then, fellow citizens, unite with one heart and one mind. Let us restore to social intercourse that harmony and affection without which liberty and even life itself are but dreary things. And let us reflect that having banished from our land that religious intolerance under which mankind so long bled and suffered, we have yet gained little if we countenance a political intolerance as despotic, as wicked, and capable of as bitter and bloody persecutions. During the throes and convulsions of the ancient world, during the agonizing spasms of infuriated man, seeking through blood and slaughter his long-lost liberty, it was not wonderful that the agitation of the billows should reach even this distant and peaceful shore; that this should be more felt and feared by some and less by others; that this should divide opinions as to measures of safety. But every difference of opinion is not a difference of principle.

We have called by different names brethren of the same principle. We are all Republicans ; we are all Federalists. If there be any among us who would wish to dissolve this Union or to change its republican form, let them stand undisturbed as monuments of the safety with which error of opinion may be tolerated where reason is left free to combat it. I know, indeed, that some honest men fear that a republican government cannot be strong; that this government is not strong enough. But would the honest patriot, in the full tide of successful experiment, abandon a government which has so far kept us free and firm, on the theoretic and visionary fear that this government, the world's best hope, may by possibility want energy to preserve itself? I trust not I believe this, on the contrary, the strongest government on earth. . . . Sometimes it is said that man cannot be trusted with the government of himself. Can he, then, be trusted with the government of others? Or have we found angels in the forms of kings to govern him? Let history answer this question.

Let us, then, with courage and confidence pursue our own federal and republican principles, our attachment to our union and representative government. Kindly separated by nature and a wide ocean from the exterminating havoc of one quarter of the globe; too high-minded to endure the degradations of the others; possessing a chosen country, with room enough for our descendants to the hundredth and thousandth generation; entertaining a due sense of our equal right to the use of our own faculties, to the acquisitions of our industry, to honor and confidence from our fellow citizens, resulting not from birth but from our actions and their sense of them; enlightened by a benign religion, professed, indeed, and practiced in various forms, yet all of them including honesty, truth, temperance, gratitude, and the love of man; acknowledging and adoring an overruling Providence, which by all its dispensations proves that it delights in the happiness of man here and his greater happiness hereafter; with all these blessings, what more is necessary to make us a happy and prosperous people? Still one thing more, fellow citizens—a wise and frugal government, which shall restrain men from injuring one another, which shall leave them otherwise free to regulate their own pursuits of industry and improvement, and shall not take from the mouth of labor the bread it has earned. This is the sum of good government, and this is necessary to close the circle of our felicities. . . .

Chapter 5

"LIBERTY AND UNION, NOW AND FOREVER"

DANIEL WEBSTER'S SECOND REPLY TO SENATOR ROBERT HAYNE, JANUARY 26, 1830

Sectional divisions were part of the nation's birth pains, but they continued even after the nation was born. Slavery, of course, was at the heart of it, but economic interests and ideology also played a role in dividing North and South. When Senator Samuel Foot of Connecticut introduced a bill to limit the sale of public lands in 1829, South Carolina Senator Robert Hayne argued that individual states had the right to declare federal laws to be null and void in their jurisdictions. Senator Daniel Webster of Massachusetts replied, and the debate between the two men quickly moved from the issue of public lands to the very nature of American democracy. The following is from Webster's second retort to Hayne, and is considered one of the greatest speeches in American political history. It was not enough, however, to heal growing divisions between North and South.

I understand the honorable gentleman from South Carolina to maintain, that it is a right of the State legislatures to interfere, whenever, in their judgment, this government transcends its constitutional limits, and to arrest the operation of its laws.

I understand him to maintain this right, as a right existing *under* the Constitution, not as a right to overthrow it on the ground of extreme necessity, such as would justify violent revolution.

I understand him to maintain an authority, on the part of the States, thus to interfere, for the purpose of correcting the exercise of power by the general government, of checking it, and of compelling it to conform to their opinion of the extent of its powers.

I understand him to maintain that the ultimate power of judging of the constitutional extent of its own authority is not lodged exclusively in the general government, or any branch of it: but that, on the contrary, the States may lawfully decide for themselves, and each State for itself, whether, in a given case, the act of the general government transcends its power.

I understand him to insist, that, if the exigency of the case, in the opinion of any State government, require it, such State government may, by its own sovereign authority, annul an act of the general government which it deems plainly and palpably unconstitutional.

This is the sum of what I understand from him to be the South Carolina doctrine, and the doctrine which he maintains. . . .

This leads us to inquire into the origin of this government and the source of its power. Whose agent is it? Is it the creature of the State legislatures, or the creature of the people? If the government of the United States be the agent of the State governments, then they may control it, provided they can agree in the manner of controlling it; if it be the agent of the people, then the people alone can control it, restrain it, modify, or reform it. It is observable enough, that the doctrine for which the honorable gentleman contends leads him to the necessity of maintaining, not only that this general government is the creature of the States, but that it is the creature of each of the States severally, so that each may assert the power for itself of determining whether it acts within the limits of its authority. It is the servant of four-and-twenty masters, of different will and different purposes and yet bound to obey all. This absurdity (for it seems no less) arises from a misconception as to the origin of this government and its true character. It is, Sir, the people's Constitution, the people's government, made for the people, made by the people, and answerable to the people. The people of the United States have declared that the Constitution shall be the supreme law. We must either admit the proposition, or dispute their authority. The States are, unquestionably, sovereign, so far as their sovereignty is not affected by this supreme law. But the State legislatures, as political bodies, however sovereign, are yet not sovereign over the people. So far as the people have given the power to the general government, so far the grant is unquestionably good, and the government holds of the people, and not of the State governments. We are all agents of the same supreme power, the people. The general government and the State governments derive their authority from the same source. . . .

I have not allowed myself, Sir, to look beyond the Union, to see what might lie hidden in the dark recess behind. I have not coolly weighed the chances of preserving liberty when the bonds that unite us together shall be broken asunder. I have not accustomed myself to hang over the precipice of disunion, to see whether, with my short sight, I can fathom the depth of the abyss below; nor could I regard him as a safe counsellor in the affairs of this government, whose thoughts should be mainly bent on considering, not how the Union may be best preserved, but how tolerable might be the condition of the people when it should be broken up and destroyed. While the Union lasts, we have high, exciting, gratifying prospects spread out before us and our children. Beyond that I seek not to penetrate the veil. God grant that in my day, at least, that curtain may not rise! God grant that on my vision never may be opened what lies behind! When my eyes shall be turned to behold for the last time the sun in heaven, may I not see him shining on the broken and dishonored fragments of a once glorious Union; on States dissevered, discordant, belligerent; on a land rent with civil feuds, or drenched, it may be, in fraternal blood! Let their last feeble and lingering glance rather behold the gorgeous ensign of the republic, now known and honored throughout the earth, still full high advanced, its arms and trophies streaming in their original luster, not a stripe erased or polluted, not a single star obscured, bearing for its motto, no such miserable interrogatory as "What is all this worth?" nor those other words of delusion and folly, "Liberty first and Union afterwards"; but everywhere, spread all over in characters of living light, blazing on all it sample folds, as they float over the sea and over the land, and in every wind under the whole heavens, that other sentiment, dear to every true American heart,—Liberty *and* Union, now and forever, one and inseparable!

Chapter 6

"THE HYPOCRISY
OF THE NATION
MUST BE EXPOSED"

FREDERICK DOUGLASS'S
INDEPENDENCE DAY SPEECH,
JULY 4, 1852

Frederick Douglass was born into slavery in Maryland in 1817. He taught himself to read and write, and in 1838, he escaped his enslaver, fleeing to Massachusetts, the center of the North's abolitionist movement. He later moved to Rochester, New York, and became renowned as a passionate voice on behalf of America's enslaved. As the nation moved ever closer to conflict over slavery, Douglass was invited by the citizens of his adopted hometown, Rochester, to deliver an oration in commemoration of Independence Day in 1852. With measured defiance and scorn, he explored the meaning of American freedom from the perspective of the nation's four million enslaved people.

Fellow citizens, pardon me, and allow me to ask, why am I called upon to speak here today? What have I or those I represent to do with your national independence? Are the great principles of political freedom and of natural justice, embodied in that Declaration of

Independence, extended to us? And am I, therefore, called upon to bring our humble offering to the national altar, and to confess the benefits, and express devout gratitude for the blessings resulting from your independence to us?

Would to God, both for your sakes and ours, that an affirmative answer could be truthfully returned to these questions. Then would my task be light, and my burden easy and delightful. . . . But such is not the state of the case. I say it with a sad sense of disparity between us. I am not included within the pale of this glorious anniversary! Your high independence only reveals the immeasurable distance between us. The blessings in which you this day rejoice are not enjoyed in common. The rich inheritance of justice, liberty, prosperity, and independence bequeathed by your fathers is shared by you, not by me. The sunlight that brought life and healing to you has brought stripes and death to me. This Fourth of July is yours, not mine. You may rejoice, I must mourn. . . .

Fellow citizens, above your national, tumultuous joy, I hear the mournful wail of millions, whose chains, heavy and grievous yesterday, are today rendered more intolerable by the jubilant shouts that reach them. . . . To forget them, to pass lightly over their wrongs and to chime in with the popular theme would be treason most scandalous and shocking, and would make me a reproach before God and the world.

My subject, then, fellow citizens, is "American Slavery." I shall see this day and its popular characteristics from the slave's point of view. Standing here, identified with the American bondman, making his wrongs mine, I do not hesitate to declare, with all my soul, that the character and conduct of this nation never looked blacker to me than on this Fourth of July.

Whether we turn to the declarations of the past, or to the professions of the present, the conduct of the nation seems equally hideous and revolting. America is false to the past, false to the present, and solemnly binds herself to be false to the future. Standing with God and the crushed and bleeding slave on this occasion, I will, in the name of humanity, which is outraged, in the name of liberty, which is fettered, in the name of the Constitution and the Bible, which are disregarded and trampled upon, dare to call in question and to denounce, with all the emphasis I can command, everything that serves to perpetuate slavery—the great sin and shame of America! "I will not equivocate—I will not excuse." I will use the severest language I can command, and yet not one word shall escape me that any man, whose judgment is not blinded by prejudice, or who is not at heart a slave-holder, shall not confess to be right and just.

But I fancy I hear some of my audience say it is just in this circumstance that you and your brother Abolitionists fail to make a favorable impression on the public mind. Would you argue more and denounce less, would you persuade more and rebuke less, your cause would be much more likely to succeed. But, I submit, where all is plain there is nothing to be argued. What point in the anti-slavery creed would you have me argue? On what branch of the subject do the people of this country need light? Must I undertake to prove that the slave is a man? That point is conceded already. Nobody doubts it. The slave-holders themselves acknowledge it in the enactment of laws for their government.

They acknowledge it when they punish disobedience on the part of the slave. . . .

What, then, remains to be argued? Is it that slavery is not divine; that God did not establish it; that our doctors of divinity are mistaken? There is blasphemy in the thought. That which is inhuman cannot be divine. Who can reason on such a proposition? They that can, may—I cannot. The time for such argument is past.

At a time like this, scorching irony, not convincing argument, is needed. Oh! Had I the ability, and could I reach the nation's ear, I would today pour out a fiery stream of biting ridicule, blasting reproach, withering sarcasm, and stern rebuke. For it is not light that is needed, but fire; it is not the gentle shower, but thunder. We need the storm, the whirlwind, and the earthquake. The feeling of the nation must be quickened; the conscience of the nation must be roused; the propriety of the nation must be startled; the hypocrisy of the nation must be exposed; and its crimes against God and man must be denounced.

What to the American slave is your Fourth of July? I answer, a day that reveals to him more than all other days of the year, the gross injustice and cruelty to which he is the constant victim. To him your celebration is a sham; your boasted liberty an unholy license; your national greatness, swelling vanity; your sounds of rejoicing are empty and heartless; your shouts of liberty and equality, hollow mock; your prayers and hymns, your sermons and thanksgivings, with all your religious parade and solemnity, are to him mere bombast, fraud, deception, impiety, and hypocrisy—a thin veil to cover up crimes which would disgrace a nation of savages. There is not a nation of the earth guilty of practices more shocking and bloody than are the people of these United States at this very hour.

Go search where you will, roam through all the monarchies and despotisms of the Old World, travel through South America, search out every abuse and when you have found the last, lay your facts by the side of the everyday practices of this nation, and you will say with me that, for revolting barbarity and shameless hypocrisy, America reigns without a rival.

Chapter 7

"THE MYSTIC CHORDS
OF MEMORY"

ABRAHAM LINCOLN'S FIRST
INAUGURAL ADDRESS, MARCH 4, 1861

🖎 No President in the nation's history has ever assumed office in more dire circumstances than Abraham
Lincoln did in 1861. During the long four-month inter-
val between his election in November 1860 and his inauguration in March, seven states seceded from the
Union. Disastrous though this was, several important
slave-holding states remained within the Union despite
fears over Lincoln's antislavery views. As he addressed
his fellow citizens on Inauguration Day, Lincoln sought
to reassure Southerners that he had no intention of
abolishing slavery where it already existed. He appealed
to the bonds which connected all Americans, regardless
of region, to the struggle for independence less than a
century earlier. Nevertheless, after South Carolina fired
on the federal garrison in Fort Sumter a month later, the
slave-holding states of Virginia, Arkansas, Tennessee,
and North Carolina followed their fellow Southerners
into the Confederate States of America.

Apprehension seems to exist among the people of
the Southern States that by the accession of a Repub-

lican administration their property and their peace and personal security are to be endangered. There has never been any reasonable cause for such apprehension. Indeed, the most ample evidence to the contrary has all the while existed and been open to their inspection. It is found in nearly all the published speeches of him who now addresses you. I do but quote from one of those speeches when I declare that "I have no purposes directly or indirectly, to interfere with the institution of slavery in the States where it exists. I believe I have no lawful right to do so, and I have no inclination to do so." Those who nominated and elected me did so with full knowledge that I had made this and many similar declarations, and had never recanted them. . . .

That there are persons in one section or another who seek to destroy the Union at all events, and are glad of any pretext to do it, I will neither affirm nor deny; but if there be such, I need address no word to them. To those, however, who really love the Union may I not speak? . . .

Physically speaking, we cannot separate. We cannot remove our respective sections from each other, nor build an impassable wall between them. A husband and wife may be divorced, and go out of the presence and beyond the reach of each other; but the different parts of our country cannot do this. . . .

My countrymen, one and all, think calmly and well upon this whole subject. Nothing valuable can be lost by taking time. If there be an object to hurry any of you in hot haste to a step which you would never take deliberately, that object will be frustrated by taking time; but no good object can be frustrated by it. Such of you as are now dissatisfied, still have the old Constitution unimpaired, and, on the sensitive point, the laws of your own framing under it; while the new administration will have no immediate power, if it would, to change either. If it were admitted that you who are dissatisfied hold the right side in the dispute, there still is no single good reason for precipitate action. Intelligence, patriotism, Christianity, and a firm reliance on Him who has never yet forsaken this favored land, are still competent to adjust in the best way all our present difficulty.

In your hands, my dissatisfied fellow-countrymen, and not in mine, is the momentous issue of civil war. The government will not assail you. You can have no conflict without being yourselves the aggressors. You have no oath registered in heaven to destroy the government, while I shall have the most solemn one to "preserve, protect, and defend it."

I am loath to close. We are not enemies, but friends. We must not be enemies. Though passion may have strained, it must not break our bonds of affection. The mystic chords of memory, stretching from every battlefield and patriot grave to every living heart and hearthstone all over this broad land, will yet swell the chorus of the Union when again touched, as surely they will be, by the better angels of our nature.

Chapter 8

"A NEW BIRTH OF FREEDOM"

LINCOLN'S GETTYSBURG ADDRESS, NOVEMBER 19, 1863

🖎 Two great armies met near a small town in Pennsylvania in July 1863. They fought with remarkable courage and determination for three days, and when it was over, the Army of Northern Virginia under Robert E. Lee was forced to retreat, leaving the Army of the Potomac bloodied but victorious. Four months later, President Lincoln traveled to the battlefield to participate in the creation of a new national cemetery on what had become hallowed ground. His short speech redefined the great conflict. The Union, he said, was engaged in a struggle not simply to preserve the nation, but to defend great principles and to bring about a new birth of freedom. With these remarks, Lincoln changed the way Americans view their terrible civil war.

Four score and seven years ago our fathers brought forth on this continent, a new nation, conceived in Liberty, and dedicated to the proposition that all men are created equal.

Now we are engaged in a great civil war, testing whether that nation, or any nation so conceived and so dedicated, can long endure. We are met on a great battlefield of that war. We have come to dedicate a portion of that field, as a final resting place for those who here gave their lives that that nation might live. It is altogether fitting and proper that we should do this.

But, in a larger sense, we can not dedicate—we can not consecrate—we can not hallow—this ground. The brave men, living and dead, who struggled here, have consecrated it, far above our poor power to add or detract. The world will little note, nor long remember what we say here, but it can never forget what they did here. It is for us the living, rather, to be dedicated here to the unfinished work which they who fought here have thus far so nobly advanced. It is rather for us to be here dedicated to the great task remaining before us— that from these honored dead we take increased devotion to that cause for which they gave the last full measure of devotion—that we here highly resolve that these dead shall not have died in vain—that this nation, under God, shall have a new birth of freedom— and that government of the people, by the people, for the people, shall not perish from the earth.

Chapter 9

"MALICE TOWARDS NONE"

ABRAHAM LINCOLN'S SECOND INAUGURAL ADDRESS, MARCH 4, 1865

☞ Peace was at hand when President Lincoln took the presidential oath of office for the second time. The Confederate cause was in disarray; the main Union force under General Ulysses Grant would soon force the surrender of Robert E. Lee and his Army of Northern Virginia. Lincoln could now look forward to victory and the reconstruction of a nation so terribly torn apart. Healing the wounds of civil war promised to be a formidable task, one which Lincoln anticipated with this eloquent plea for a just, lasting, and authentic peace between North and South. Lincoln, of course, did not live to preside over the nation's return to peace. He was assassinated just over a month after giving this speech, on April 15, 1865.

On the occasion corresponding to this four years ago all thoughts were anxiously directed to an impending civil war. All dreaded it, all sought to avert it. While the inaugural address was being delivered from this place, devoted altogether to saving the Union without war, insurgent agents were in the city seeking to destroy it without war—seeking to dissolve the Union and divide effects by negotiation. Both parties deprecated war, but one of them would make war rather than let the nation survive, and the other would accept war rather than let it perish, and the war came.

One eighth of the whole population was colored slaves, not distributed generally over the Union, but localized in the southern part of it. These slaves constituted a peculiar and powerful interest. All knew that this interest was somehow the cause of the war. To strengthen, perpetuate, and extend this interest was the object for which the insurgents would rend the Union even by war, while the Government claimed no right to do more than to restrict the territorial enlargement of it. Neither party expected for the war the magnitude or the duration which it has already attained. Neither anticipated that the cause of the conflict might cease with or even before the conflict itself should cease. Each looked for an easier triumph, and a result less fundamental and astounding. Both read the same Bible and pray to the same God, and each invokes his aid against the other. It may seem strange that any men should dare to ask a just God's assistance in wringing their bread from the sweat of other men's faces, but let us judge not, that we be not judged. The prayers of both could not be answered. That of neither has been answered fully. The Almighty has his own purposes. . . . Fondly do we hope, fervently do we pray, that this mighty scourge of war may speedily pass away. Yet, if God wills that it continue until all the wealth piled by the bondsman's two hundred and fifty years of unrequited toil shall be sunk, and until every drop of blood drawn with the lash shall be paid by another drawn with the sword, as was said three thousand years ago, so still it must be said, "The judgments of the Lord are true and righteous altogether."

With malice towards none, with charity for all, with firmness in the right as God gives us to see the right, let us strive on to finish the work we are in, to bind up the nation's wounds, to care for him who shall have borne the battle and for his widow and his orphan, to do all which may achieve and cherish a just and lasting peace among ourselves and with all nations.

■||||||||||||||||||||||||||||||||||||||||||■

Chapter 10

"A CROSS OF GOLD"

■||||||||||||||||||||||||||||||||||||||||||■

WILLIAM JENNINGS BRYAN'S SPEECH AT THE DEMOCRATIC NATIONAL CONVENTION IN CHICAGO, JULY 9, 1896

☞ Times were difficult in the 1890s—unemployment was high following a financial panic in 1893, and farmers and workers sought to loosen financial restrictions through the free coinage of silver-based currency. Business leaders insisted that the nation adhere to the gold standard, which limited the supply of money and led to tighter credit. On the second day of the Democratic National Convention in 1896, a thirty-six-year-old former congressman from Nebraska named William Jennings Bryan delivered this fiery speech which condemned the business elites of New York and Boston—including those in his own party. Bryan's speech electrified the convention and led to his nomination as the party's presidential candidate. Bryan, however, lost the 1896 election—and two more presidential elections (1900 and 1908) after that. But his speech remains among the most famous in American political history.

On the 4th of March, 1895, a few Democrats, most of them members of Congress, issued an address to the

Democrats of the nation asserting that the money question was the paramount issue of the hour; asserting also the right of a majority of the Democratic Party to control the position of the party on this paramount issue; concluding with the request that all believers in free coinage of silver in the Democratic Party should organize and take charge of and control the policy of the Democratic Party. Three months later, at Memphis, an organization was perfected, and the silver Democrats went forth openly and boldly and courageously proclaiming their belief and declaring that if successful they would crystallize in a platform the declaration which they had made; and then began the conflict with a zeal approaching the zeal which inspired the crusaders who followed Peter the Hermit. Our silver Democrats went forth from victory unto victory, until they are assembled now, not to discuss, not to debate, but to enter up the judgment rendered by the plain people of this country.

But in this contest, brother has been arrayed against brother, and father against son. The warmest ties of love and acquaintance and association have been disregarded. Old leaders have been cast aside when they refused to give expression to the sentiments of those whom they would lead, and new leaders have sprung up to give direction to this cause of freedom. Thus has the contest been waged, and we have assembled here under as binding and solemn instructions as were ever fastened upon the representatives of a people. . . .

When you come before us and tell us that we shall disturb your business interests, we reply that you have disturbed our business interests by your action. We say to you that you have made too limited in its application the definition of a businessman. The man who is employed for wages is as much a businessman as his employer. The attorney in a country town is as much a businessman as the corporation counsel in a great metropolis. The merchant at the crossroads store is as much a businessman as the merchant of New York. The farmer who goes forth in the morning and toils all day, begins in the spring and toils all summer, and by the application of brain and muscle to the natural resources of this country creates wealth, is as much a businessman as the man who goes upon the Board of Trade and bets upon the price of grain. The miners who go 1,000 feet into the earth or climb 2,000 feet upon the cliffs and bring forth from their hiding places the precious metals to be poured in the channels of trade are as much businessmen as the few financial magnates who in a backroom corner the money of the world.

We come to speak for this broader class of businessmen. Ah, my friends, we say not one word against those who live upon the Atlantic Coast; but those hardy pioneers who braved all the dangers of the wilderness, who have made the desert to blossom as the rose—those pioneers away out there, rearing their children near to nature's heart, where they can mingle their voices with the voices of the birds—out there where they have erected schoolhouses for the education of their children and churches where they praise their Creator, and the cemeteries where sleep the ashes of their dead—are as deserving of the consideration of this party as any people in this country.

It is for these that we speak. We do not come as aggressors. Our war is not a war of conquest. We are fighting in the defense of our homes, our families, and posterity. We have petitioned, and our petitions have been scorned. We have entreated, and our entreaties have been disregarded. We have begged, and they have mocked when our calamity came.

We beg no longer; we entreat no more; we petition no more. We defy them! . . .

There are two ideas of government. There are those who believe that if you just legislate to make the well-to-do prosperous, that their prosperity will leak through on those below. The Democratic idea has been that if you legislate to make the masses prosperous their prosperity will find its way up and through every class that rests upon it.

You come to us and tell us that the great cities are in favor of the gold standard. I tell you that the great cities rest upon these broad and fertile prairies. Burn down your cities and leave our farms, and your cities will spring up again as if by magic. But destroy our farms and the grass will grow in the streets of every city in the country. . . .

If they dare to come out in the open field and defend the gold standard as a good thing, we shall fight them to the uttermost, having behind us the producing masses of the nation and the world. Having behind us the commercial interests and the laboring interests and all the toiling masses, we shall answer their demands for a gold standard by saying to them, you shall not press down upon the brow of labor this crown of thorns. You shall not crucify mankind upon a cross of gold.

Chapter 11

"CORPORATIONS . . .
SHOULD BE
REGULATED"

THEODORE ROOSEVELT'S SPEECH ON
THE NATION'S TRUSTS,
DECEMBER 3, 1901

☞ The ascension of Theodore Roosevelt to the presidency in 1901 marked the beginning of a new era of change and reform. In this speech, Roosevelt outlined a new, more aggressive policy designed to monitor and regulate the era's largest companies and industries, known as "trusts." He proposed the creation of a Department of Commerce and Industries, which became the current Department of Commerce. Roosevelt's insistence that the federal government had a right and a duty to regulate and supervise large corporations engaged in interstate commerce was a milestone in American political history. Roosevelt effectively ended the nation's adherence to nineteenth-century ideas of laissez-faire economics and opened the way for a much greater government presence in the nation's economy.

There is a widespread conviction in the minds of the American people that the great corporations known as trusts are in certain of their features and tendencies hurtful to the general welfare. This springs from no spirit of envy or uncharitableness, nor lack of pride in the great industrial achievements that have placed this country at the head of the nations struggling for commercial supremacy. It does not rest upon a lack of intelligent appreciation of the necessity of meeting changing and changed conditions of trade with new methods, nor upon ignorance of the fact that combination of capital in the effort to accomplish great things is necessary when the world's progress demands that great things be done. It is based upon sincere conviction that combination and concentration should be, not prohibited, but supervised and within reasonable limits controlled; and in my judgment this conviction is right.

It is no limitation upon property rights or freedom of contract to require that when men receive from Government the privilege of doing business under corporate form, which frees them from individual responsibility, and enables them to call into their enterprises the capital of the public, they shall do so upon absolutely truthful representations as to the value of the property in which the capital is to be invested. Corporations engaged in interstate commerce should be regulated if they are found to exercise a license working to the public injury. It should be as much the aim of those who seek for social-betterment to rid the business world of crimes of cunning as to rid the entire body politic of crimes of violence. Great corporations exist only because they are created and safeguarded by our institutions; and it is therefore our right and our duty to see that they work in harmony with these institutions.

The first essential in determining how to deal with the

great industrial combinations is knowledge of the facts—
publicity. In the interest of the public, the Government should have the right to inspect and examine the
workings of the great corporations engaged in interstate
business. Publicity is the only sure remedy which we can
now invoke. What further remedies are needed in the
way of governmental regulation, or taxation, can only
be determined after publicity has been obtained, by process of law, and in the course of administration. . . .

The large corporations, commonly called trusts,
though organized in one State, always do business in
many States, often doing very little business in the
State where they are incorporated. There is utter lack of
uniformity in the State laws about them; and as no
State has any exclusive interest in or power over their
acts, it has in practice proved impossible to get adequate regulation through State action. Therefore, in the
interest of the whole people, the Nation should, without interfering with the power of the States in the matter itself, also assume power of supervision and
regulation over all corporations doing an interstate
business. This is especially true where the corporation
derives a portion of its wealth from the existence of
some monopolistic element or tendency in its business.
There would be no hardship in such supervision; banks
are subject to it, and in their case it is now accepted as
a simple matter of course. Indeed, it is probable that
supervision of corporations by the National Government need not go so far as is now the case with the
supervision exercised over them by so conservative a
State as Massachusetts, in order to produce excellent
results.

When the Constitution was adopted, at the end of

the eighteenth century, no human wisdom could foretell the sweeping changes, alike in industrial and political conditions, which were to take place by the beginning of the twentieth century. At that time it was accepted as a matter of course that the several States were the proper authorities to regulate, so far as was then necessary, the comparatively insignificant and strictly localized corporate bodies of the day. The conditions are now wholly different and wholly different action is called for. I believe that a law can be framed which will enable the National Government to exercise control along the lines above indicated; profiting by the experience gained through the passage and administration of the Interstate-Commerce Act. If, however, the judgment of the Congress is that it lacks the constitutional power to pass such an act, then a constitutional amendment should be submitted to confer the power.

There should be created a Cabinet officer, to be known as Secretary of Commerce and Industries, as provided in the bill introduced at the last session of the Congress. It should be his province to deal with commerce in its broadest sense; including among many other things whatever concerns labor and all matters affecting the great business corporations and our merchant marine. . . .

The most vital problem with which this country, and for that matter the whole civilized world, has to deal, is the problem which has for one side the betterment of social conditions, moral and physical, in large cities, and for another side the effort to deal with that tangle of far-reaching questions which we group together when we speak of "labor." The chief factor in the success of each man—wage-worker, farmer, and capitalist alike—must ever be the sum total of his own individual qualities and abilities. Second only to this comes the power of acting in combination or association with others. Very great good has been and will be accomplished by associations or unions of wage-workers, when managed with forethought, and when they combine insistence upon their own rights with law-abiding respect for the rights of others. The display of these qualities in such bodies is a duty to the nation no less than to the associations themselves. . . .

When all is said and done, the rule of brotherhood remains as the indispensable prerequisite to success in the kind of national life for which we strive. Each man must work for himself, and unless he so works no outside help can avail him; but each man must remember also that he is indeed his brother's keeper, and that while no man who refuses to walk can be carried with advantage to himself or anyone else, yet that each at times stumbles or halts, that each at times needs to have the helping hand outstretched to him. To be permanently effective, aid must always take the form of helping a man to help himself; and we can all best help ourselves by joining together in the work that is of common interest to all. . . .

Chapter 12

"THE MAN WITH THE MUCK RAKE"

THEODORE ROOSEVELT'S PLEA FOR CIVIL DISCOURSE, APRIL 15, 1906

☞ Theodore Roosevelt was an ally of many of the crusading journalists whose stories about corporate excesses, social inequality, and political corruption helped to change American politics in the early twentieth century. But as newspapers and magazines printed increasingly vehement attacks on business leaders and politicians, Roosevelt grew uncomfortable with the personal tone of these journalistic crusaders. Several weeks before this speech, for example, *Cosmopolitan* magazine published a scathing piece by journalist David Graham Phillips which bore the sensational headline, "The Treason of the Senate." In this speech, Roosevelt acknowledged the need to expose wrong, but argued that journalists should not be blind to the nation's better attributes. Roosevelt helped coin the term "muckrakers" with his reference to a character in the novel *Pilgrim's Progress*.

In Bunyan's *Pilgrim's Progress* you may recall the description of the Man with the Muck Rake, the man who could look no way but downward, with the muck rake in his hand; who was offered a celestial crown for his muck rake, but who would neither look up nor regard the crown he was offered, but continued to rake to himself the filth of the floor.

In *Pilgrim's Progress* the Man with the Muck Rake is set forth as the example of him whose vision is fixed on carnal instead of spiritual things. Yet he also typifies the man who in this life consistently refuses to see aught that is lofty, and fixes his eyes with solemn intentness only on that which is vile and debasing.

Now, it is very necessary that we should not flinch from seeing what is vile and debasing. There is filth on the floor, and it must be scraped up with the muck rake; and there are times and places where this service is the most needed of all the services that can be performed. But the man who never does anything else, who never thinks or speaks or writes, save of his feats with the muck rake, speedily becomes, not a help but one of the most potent forces for evil.

There are in the body politic, economic and social, many and grave evils, and there is urgent necessity for the sternest war upon them. There should be relentless exposure of and attack upon every evil man, whether politician or business man, every evil practice, whether in politics, business, or social life. I hail as a benefactor every writer or speaker, every man who, on the platform or in a book, magazine, or newspaper, with merciless severity makes such attack, provided always that he in his turn remembers that the attack is of use only if it is absolutely truthful.

The liar is no whit better than the thief, and if his mendacity takes the form of slander he may be worse than most thieves. It puts a premium upon knavery untruthfully to attack an honest man, or even with hysterical exaggeration to assail a bad man with untruth.

An epidemic of indiscriminate assault upon character does no good, but very great harm. The soul of every scoundrel is gladdened whenever an honest man is assailed, or even when a scoundrel is untruthfully assailed.

Now, it is easy to twist out of shape what I have just said, easy to affect to misunderstand it, and if it is slurred over in repetition not difficult really to misunderstand it. Some persons are sincerely incapable of understanding that to denounce mud slinging does not mean the endorsement of whitewashing; and both the interested individuals who need whitewashing and those others who practice mud slinging like to encourage such confusion of ideas. . . .

It is because I feel that there should be no rest in the endless war against the forces of evil that I ask the war be conducted with sanity as well as with resolution. The men with the muck rakes are often indispensable to the well being of society; but only if they know when to stop raking the muck, and to look upward to the celestial crown above them, to the crown of worthy endeavor. There are beautiful things above and round about them; and if they gradually grow to feel that the whole world is nothing but muck, their power of usefulness is gone.

If the whole picture is painted black there remains no hue whereby to single out the rascals for distinction from their fellows. Such painting finally induces a kind of moral color blindness; and people affected by it come to the conclusion that no man is really black, and no man really white, but they are all gray. . . .

Hysterical sensationalism is the poorest weapon wherewith to fight for lasting righteousness. The men who with stern sobriety and truth assail the many evils of our time, whether in the public press, or in magazines, or in books, are the leaders and allies of all engaged in the work for social and political betterment. But if they give good reason for distrust of what they say, if they chill the ardor of those who demand truth as a primary virtue, they thereby betray the good cause and play into the hands of the very men against whom they are nominally at war. . . .

The foundation stone of national life is, and ever must be, the high individual character of the average citizen.

Chapter 13

"THE WOMAN'S HOUR HAS STRUCK"

CARRIE CHAPMAN CATT'S SPEECH IN ATLANTA ON WOMEN'S RIGHTS, SEPTEMBER 7, 1916

A catastrophic world war was underway when Carrie Chapman Catt, one of the nation's best-known advocates of women's suffrage, addressed an audience of supporters in Atlanta in 1916. Catt saw the war, which already had cost the lives of millions, as a key moment for the women's movement. After the war, she predicted, women in Europe would refuse to return to their traditional places outside the public square. American women, as yet unaffected by the war (the United States was neutral at the time) would inevitably demand the same rights which Europe's women were demanding. Victory, she cautioned, would be difficult, for it would require the participation of all women, including those who were content to let others do the tedious work of political organizing. Now was the time, she said. She was not wrong. Women in the United States won the right to vote in federal elections in 1920, with the passage of the Nineteenth Amendment.

I have taken for my subject, "The Crisis," because I believe that a crisis has come in our movement which, if recognized and the opportunity seized with vigor, enthusiasm and will, means the final victory of our great cause in the very near future. I am aware that some suffragists do not share this belief; they see no signs nor symptoms today which were not present yesterday; no manifestations in the year 1916 which differ significantly from those in the year 1910. To them, the movement has been a steady, normal growth from the beginning and must so continue until the end. I can only defend my claim with the plea that it is better to imagine a crisis where none exists than to fail to recognize one when it comes; for a crisis is a culmination of events which calls for new considerations and new decisions. A failure to answer the call may mean an opportunity lost, a possible victory postponed. . . .

Therefore, fellow suffragists, I invite your attention to the signs which point to a crisis and your consideration of plans for turning the crisis into victory.

First, we are passing through a world crisis. All thinkers of every land tell us so; and that nothing after the great war will be as it was before. Those who profess to know, claim that 100 millions of dollars are being spent on the war every day and that two years of war have cost 50 billions of dollars or 10 times more than the total expense of the American Civil War. Our own country has sent 35 millions of dollars abroad for relief expenses. . . .

The stability of human institutions has never before suffered so tremendous a shock. Great men are trying to think out the consequences but one and all proclaim that no imagination can find color or form bold enough to paint the picture of the world after the war. British and Russian, German and Austrian, French and Italian agree that it will lead to social and political revolution throughout the entire world. Whatever comes, they further agree that the war presages a total change in the status of women. . . .

What then, will happen after the war? Will the widows left with families to support cheerfully leave their well-paid posts for those commanding lower wages? Not without protest! Will the wives who now must support crippled husbands give up their skilled work and take up the occupations which were open to them before the war? Will they resignedly say: "The woman who has a healthy husband who can earn for her, has a right to tea and raisin cake, but the woman who earns for herself and a husband who has given his all to his country, must be content with butterless bread"?

Not without protest!

On the contrary, the economic axiom, denied and evaded for centuries, will be blazoned on every factory, counting house and shop: "Equal pay for equal work"; and common justice will slowly, but surely enforce that law. . . .

"The Woman's Hour has struck." It has struck for the women of Europe and for those of all the world. The significance of the changed status of European women has not been lost upon the men and women of our land; our own people are not so unlearned in history, nor so lacking in National pride that they will allow the Republic to lag long behind the Empire, presided over by the descendant of George the Third. If they possess the patriotism and the sense of nationality which should be the inheritance of an American, they will not wait until the war is ended but will boldly lead in the inevitable march of democracy, our own American specialty. . . .

Before the vote is won, there must and will be a gigantic final conflict between the forces of progress, righteousness and democracy and the forces of ignorance, evil and reaction. That struggle may be postponed, but it cannot be evaded or avoided. There is no question as to which side will be the victor. . . .

Are we prepared to grasp the victory? Alas, no! Our movement is like a great Niagara with a vast volume of water tumbling over its ledge but turning no wheel. Our organized machinery is set for the propagandistic stage and not for the seizure of victory. Our supporters are spreading the argument for our cause; they feel no sense of responsibility for the realization of our hopes. Our movement lacks cohesion, organization, unity and consequent momentum.

Behind us, in front of us, everywhere about us are suffragists—millions of them, but inactive and silent. They have been "agitated and educated" and are with us in belief. There are thousands of women who have at one time or another been members of our organization but they have dropped out because, to them the movement seemed negative and pointless. Many have taken up other work whose results were more immediate. Philanthropy, charity, work for corrective laws of various kinds, temperance, relief for working women and numberless similar public services have called them. Others have turned to the pleasanter avenues of clubwork, art or literature. . . .

If you believe with me that a crisis has come to our movement—if you believe that the time for final action is now, if you catch the rosy tints of the coming day, what does it mean to you? Does it not give you a thrill of exaltation; does the blood not course more quickly

Chapter 14

"THE MOST IMPORTANT QUESTION IN THIS COUNTRY TODAY"

SENATOR ROBERT LA FOLLETTE'S DEFENSE OF WARTIME DISSENT, OCTOBER 6, 1917

The United States was swept up in war fever in 1917, but some skeptics, including Wisconsin senator Robert La Follette, questioned the wisdom of American involvement in the great conflict that became known as World War I. Many found themselves condemned as traitors and subversives. As troops prepared to sail "over there" to fight and die in the trenches of France, La Follette came to the defense of dissent in a speech on the Senate floor. La Follette argued that free speech could not be suspended even in a time of war, that dissent in wartime was not a crime. La Follette did not simply defend the right of dissenters to speak freely in wartime. Addressing himself to the president of the Senate, La Follette also assailed those who would shut down debate, arguing, in essence, that they, too, were the enemies of democracy.

I have no intention of taking the time of the Senate with a review of the events which led to our entrance into the war except in so far as they bear upon the question of personal privilege to which I am addressing myself.

Six members of the Senate and 50 members of the House voted against the declaration of war. Immediately there was let loose upon those Senators and Representatives a flood of invective and abuse from newspapers and individuals who had been clamoring for war, unequaled, I believe, in the history of civilized society.

Prior to the declaration of war every man who had ventured to oppose our entrance into it had been condemned as a coward or worse, and even the President had by no means been immune from these attacks.

Since the declaration of war the triumphant war press has pursued those Senators and Representatives who voted against war with malicious falsehood and recklessly libelous attacks, going to the extreme limit of charging them with treason against their country.

This campaign of libel and character assassination directed against the Members of Congress who opposed our entrance into the war has been continued down to the present hour, and I have upon my desk newspaper clippings, some of them libels upon me alone, some directed as well against other Senators who voted in opposition to the declaration of war. . . .

But, sir, it is not alone Members of Congress that the war party in this country has sought to intimidate. The mandate seems to have gone forth to the sovereign people of this country that they must be silent while those things are being done by their Government which most vitally concern their well-being, their happiness, and their lives. Today and for weeks past honest and law-abiding citizens of this country are being terrorized and outraged in their rights by those sworn to uphold the laws and protect the rights of the people. I have in my possession numerous affidavits establishing the fact that people are being unlawfully arrested, thrown into jail, held incommunicado for days, only to be eventually discharged without ever having been taken into court, because they have committed no crime. Private residences are being invaded, loyal citizens of undoubted integrity and probity arrested, cross-examined, and the most sacred constitutional rights guaranteed to every American citizen are being violated.

It appears to be the purpose of those conducting this campaign to throw the country into a state of terror, to coerce public opinion, to stifle criticism, and suppress discussion of the great issues involved in this war.

I think all men recognize that in time of war the citizen must surrender some rights for the common good which he is entitled to enjoy in time of peace. But sir, the right to control their own Government according to constitutional forms is not one of the rights that the citizens of this country are called upon to surrender in time of war.

Rather in time of war the citizen must be more alert to the preservation of his right to control his Government. He must be most watchful of the encroachment of the military upon the civil power. He must beware of those precedents in support of arbitrary action by administrative officials, which excused on the plea of necessity in war time, become the fixed rule when the necessity has passed and normal conditions have been restored.

More than all, the citizen and his representative in Congress in time of war must maintain his right of free speech. More than in times of peace it is necessary that the channels for free public discussion of governmental policies shall be open and unclogged. I believe, Mr. President, that I am now touching upon the most important question in this country today—and that is the right of the citizens of this country and their representatives in Congress to discuss in an orderly way frankly and publicly and without fear, from the platform and through the press, every important phase of this war; its causes, the manner in which it should be conducted, and the terms upon which peace should be made. The belief which is becoming wide spread in this land that this most fundamental right is being denied to the citizens of this country is a fact the tremendous significance of which, those in authority have not yet begun to appreciate. I am contending, Mr. President, for the great fundamental right of the sovereign people of this country to make their voice heard and have that voice heeded upon the great questions arising out of this war, including not only how the war shall be prosecuted but the conditions upon which it may be terminated with a due regard for the rights and the honor of this Nation and the interests of humanity.

I am contending for this right because the exercise of it is necessary to the welfare, to the existence, of this Government, to the successful conduct of this war, and to a peace which shall be enduring and for the best interest of this country.

Suppose success attends the attempt to stifle all discussion of the issues of this war, all discussion of the terms upon which it should be concluded, all discussion of the objects and purposes to be accomplished by it, and concede the demand of the war-mad press and war extremists that they monopolize the right of public utterance upon these questions unchallenged, what think you would be the consequences to this country not only during the war but after the war? . . .

It is no answer to say that when the war is over the citizen may once more resume his rights and feel some security in his liberty and his person. As I have already tried to point out, now is precisely the time when the country needs the counsel of all its citizens. In time of war even more than in time of peace, whether citizens happen to agree with the ruling administration or not, these precious fundamental personal rights—free speech, free press, and right of assemblage so explicitly and emphatically guaranteed by the Constitution should be maintained inviolable. . . .

Chapter 15

"THE CULMINATING AND FINAL WAR FOR HUMAN LIBERTY"

**PRESIDENT WOODROW WILSON
ENUNCIATES HIS FOURTEEN POINTS
TO CONGRESS, JANUARY 8, 1918.**

☞ President Wilson changed the meaning of World War I by attaching a moral purpose to the bloody catastrophe that cost the lives of millions. It was Wilson who framed the war as a way to make the world safe for democracy, as a means to bring about the end of war. More formally, in early 1918, Wilson presented to Congress his vision of the war's aims. As a statement of uniquely American idealism and optimism at a terrible time in world history, Wilson's fourteen-points speech endowed the war with a nobility that was difficult to discern in the rat-infested trenches of Flanders.

We entered this war because violations of right had occurred which touched us to the quick and made the life of our own people impossible unless they were corrected and the world secure once for all against their recurrence. What we demand in this war, therefore, is nothing peculiar to ourselves. It is that the world be made fit and safe to live in; and particularly that it be made safe for every peace-loving nation which, like our own, wishes to live its own life, determine its own institutions, be assured of justice and fair dealing by the other peoples of the world as against force and selfish aggression. All the peoples of the world are in effect partners in this interest, and for our own part we see very clearly that unless justice be done to others it will not be done to us. The program of the world's peace, therefore, is our program; and that program, the only possible program, as we see it, is this:

I. Open covenants of peace, openly arrived at, after which there shall be no private international understandings of any kind but diplomacy shall proceed always frankly and in the public view.

II. Absolute freedom of navigation upon the seas, outside territorial waters, alike in peace and in war, except as the seas may be closed in whole or in part by international action for the enforcement of international covenants.

III. The removal, so far as possible, of all economic barriers and the establishment of an equality of trade conditions among all the nations consenting to the peace and associating themselves for its maintenance.

IV. Adequate guarantees given and taken that national armaments will be reduced to the lowest point consistent with domestic safety.

V. A free, open-minded, and absolutely impartial adjustment of all colonial claims, based upon a strict observance of the principle that in determining all such questions of sovereignty the interests of the populations concerned must have equal weight with the equitable claims of the government whose title is to be determined.

VI. The evacuation of all Russian territory and such a settlement of all questions affecting Russia as will secure the best and freest cooperation of the other nations of the world in obtaining for her an unhampered and unembarrassed opportunity for the independent determination of her own political development and national policy and assure her of a sincere welcome into the society of free nations under institutions of her own choosing; and, more than a welcome, assistance also of every kind that she may need and may herself desire. The treatment accorded Russia by her sister nations in the months to come will be the acid test of their good will, of their comprehension of her needs as distinguished from their own interests, and of their intelligent and unselfish sympathy.

VII. Belgium, the whole world will agree, must be evacuated and restored, without any attempt to limit the sovereignty which she enjoys in common with all other free nations. No other single act will serve as this will serve to restore confidence among the nations in the laws which they have themselves set and determined for the government of their relations with one another. Without this healing act the whole structure and validity of international law is forever impaired.

VIII. All French territory should be freed and the invaded portions restored, and the wrong done to France by Prussia in 1871 in the matter of Alsace-Lorraine, which has unsettled the peace of the world for nearly fifty years, should be righted, in order that peace may once more be made secure in the interest of all.

IX. A readjustment of the frontiers of Italy should be effected along clearly recognizable lines of nationality.

X. The peoples of Austria-Hungary, whose place among the nations we wish to see safeguarded and assured, should be accorded the freest opportunity to autonomous development.

XI. Rumania, Serbia, and Montenegro should be evacuated; occupied territories restored; Serbia accorded free and secure access to the sea; and the relations of the several Balkan states to one another determined by friendly counsel along historically established lines of allegiance and nationality; and international guarantees of the political and economic independence and territorial integrity of the several Balkan states should be entered into.

XII. The Turkish portion of the present Ottoman Empire should be assured a secure sovereignty, but the other nationalities which are now under Turkish rule should be assured an undoubted security of life and an absolutely unmolested opportunity of autonomous development, and the Dardanelles should be permanently opened as a free passage to the ships and commerce of all nations under international guarantees.

XIII. An independent Polish state should be erected which should include the territories inhabited by indisputably Polish populations, which should be assured a free and secure access to the sea, and whose political and economic independence and territorial integrity should be guaranteed by international covenant.

XIV. A general association of nations must be

formed under specific covenants for the purpose of affording mutual guarantees of political independence and territorial integrity to great and small states alike. . . .

We have spoken now, surely, in terms too concrete to admit of any further doubt or question. An evident principle runs through the whole program I have outlined. It is the principle of justice to all peoples and nationalities, and their right to live on equal terms of liberty and safety with one another, whether they be strong or weak. . . .

Chapter 16

"NOTHING TO FEAR
BUT FEAR ITSELF"

FRANKLIN D. ROOSEVELT'S FIRST
INAUGURAL ADDRESS, MARCH 4, 1933

As Franklin Roosevelt took the oath of office as President in 1933, tens of millions were out of work, ruined, living in parks, and lining up for handouts of bread and soup. The Great Depression, which began with a catastrophic stock market crash in 1929, provided a terrifying backdrop to FDR's inauguration. In this speech, heard around the country thanks to the amazing new technology of radio, FDR famously sought to assure an anxious nation that fear was, in fact, their greatest fear. But the speech also went on to condemn the "stubbornness" and "incompetence" of the "rulers of the exchange." Inaugural Addresses generally seek to bring together Americans after an election. This speech, however, sharply criticized those who, in FDR's view, were responsible for the economic catastrophe.

I am certain that my fellow Americans expect that on my induction into the Presidency I will address them with a candor and a decision which the present situation of our Nation impels. This is preeminently the time to speak the truth, the whole truth, frankly and boldly. Nor need we shrink from honestly facing conditions in our country to-day. This great Nation will endure as it has endured, will revive and will prosper. So, first of all, let me assert my firm belief that the only thing we have to fear is fear itself—nameless, unreasoning unjustified terror which paralyzes needed efforts to convert retreat into advance. In every dark hour of our national life a leadership of frankness and vigor has met with that understanding and support of the people themselves which is essential to victory. I am convinced that you will again give that support to leadership in these critical days.

In such a spirit on my part and on yours we face our common difficulties. They concern, thank God, only material things. Values have shrunken to fantastic levels; taxes have risen; our ability to pay has fallen; government of all kinds is faced by serious curtailment of income; the means of exchange are frozen in the currents of trade; the withered leaves of industrial enterprise lie on every side; farmers find no markets for their produce; the savings of many years in thousands of families are gone.

More important, a host of unemployed citizens face the grim problem of existence, and an equally great number toil with little return. Only a foolish optimist can deny the dark realities of the moment.

Yet our distress comes from no failure of substance. We are stricken by no plague of locusts. Compared with the perils which our forefathers conquered because they believed and were not afraid, we have still much to be thankful for. Nature still offers her bounty and human efforts have multiplied it. Plenty is at our doorstep, but a generous use of it languishes in the very sight of the supply.

Primarily this is because the rulers of the exchange of mankind's goods have failed, through their own stubbornness and their own incompetence, have admitted their failure, and abdicated. Practices of the unscrupulous money changers stand indicted in the court of public opinion, rejected by the hearts and minds of men. True they have tried, but their efforts have been cast in the pattern of an outworn tradition. Faced by failure of credit they have proposed only the lending of more money. Stripped of the lure of profit by which to induce our people to follow their false leadership, they have resorted to exhortations, pleading tearfully for restored confidence. They know only the rules of a generation of self-seekers. They have no vision, and when there is no vision the people perish.

The money changers have fled from their high seats in the temple of our civilization. We may now restore that temple to the ancient truths. The measure of the restoration lies in the extent to which we apply social values more noble than mere monetary profit.

Happiness lies not in the mere possession of money; it lies in the joy of achievement, in the thrill of creative effort. The joy and moral stimulation of work no longer must be forgotten in the mad chase of evanescent profits. These dark days will be worth all they cost us if they teach us that our true destiny is not to be ministered unto but to minister to ourselves and to our fellow men. . . .

Restoration calls, however, not for changes in ethics alone. This Nation asks for action, and action now. Our greatest primary task is to put people to work. This is no unsolvable problem if we face it wisely and courageously. It can be accomplished in part by direct recruiting by the Government itself, treating the task as we would treat the emergency of a war, but at the same time, through this employment, accomplishing greatly needed projects to stimulate and reorganize the use of our natural resources. . . .

If I read the temper of our people correctly, we now realize as we have never realized before our interdependence on each other; that we can not merely take but we must give as well; that if we are to go forward, we must move as a trained and loyal army willing to sacrifice for the good of a common discipline, because without such discipline no progress is made, no leadership becomes effective. We are, I know, ready and willing to submit our lives and property to such discipline, because it makes possible a leadership which aims at a larger good. This I propose to offer, pledging that the larger purposes will bind upon us all as a sacred obligation with a unity of duty hitherto evoked only in time of armed strife. ...

We face the arduous days that lie before us in the warm courage of the national unity; with the clear consciousness of seeking old and precious moral values; with the clean satisfaction that comes from the stern performance of duty by old and young alike. We aim at the assurance of a rounded and permanent national life. We do not distrust the future of essential democracy. The people of the United States have not failed. In their need they have registered a mandate that they want direct, vigorous action. They have asked for discipline and direction under leadership. They have made me the present instrument of their wishes. In the spirit of the gift I take it. . . .

Chapter 17

"EVERY MAN A KING"

SENATOR HUEY LONG'S RADIO
ADDRESS, FEBRUARY 23, 1934

🖙 Huey Long was the political boss of his home state of Louisiana, and one of the most colorful and controversial American politicians of the twentieth century. Elected to the U.S. Senate in 1932, Long initially supported Franklin Roosevelt's New Deal but soon grew dissatisfied with the pace and scope of reform. Long decided to challenge FDR with a radical reform program of his own. Speaking to a national radio audience less than a year after FDR's inauguration, Long unveiled a plan of economic redistribution he called "Share Our Wealth." The plan's motto was "every man a king." Long became a persistent critic of FDR and was considered a possible challenger for the Democratic presidential nomination in 1936, but his national ambitions came to an end when he was assassinated in Louisiana in September 1935.

I contend, my friends, that we have no difficult problem to solve in America, and that is the view of nearly everyone with whom I have discussed the matter here in Washington and elsewhere throughout the United States—that we have no very difficult problem to solve.

It is not the difficulty of the problem which we have; it is the fact that the rich people of this country—and by rich people I mean the super-rich—will not allow us to solve the problems, or rather the one little problem that is afflicting this country, because in order to cure all of our woes it is necessary to scale down the big fortunes, that we may scatter the wealth to be shared by all of the people. . . .

It is necessary to save the Government of the country, but is much more necessary to save the people of America. We love this country. We love this Government. It is a religion, I say. It is a kind of religion people have read of when women, in the name of religion, would take their infant babes and throw them into the burning flame, where they would be instantly devoured by the all-consuming fire, in days gone by; and there probably are some people of the world even today, who, in the name of religion, throw their tear-dimmed eyes into the sad faces of their fathers and mothers, who cannot give them food and clothing they both needed, and which is necessary to sustain them, and that goes on day after day, and night after night, when day gets into darkness and blackness, knowing those children would arise in the morning without being fed, and probably go to bed at night without being fed.

Yet in the name of our Government, and all alone, those people undertake and strive as hard as they can to keep a good government alive, and how long they can stand that no one knows. If I were in their place tonight, the place where millions are, I hope that I would have what I might say—I cannot give you the word to express the kind of fortitude they have; that is the word—I hope that I might have the fortitude to praise and honor my Government that had allowed me here in this land, where there is too much to eat and too much to wear, to starve in order that a handful of men can have so much more than they can ever eat or they can ever wear.

Now, we have organized a society, and we call it "Share Our Wealth Society," a society with the motto "every man a king."

Every man a king, so there would be no such thing as a man or woman who did not have the necessities of life, who would not be dependent upon the whims and caprices . . . of the financial martyrs for a living. What do we propose by this society? We propose to limit the wealth of big men in the country. There is an average of $15,000 in wealth to every family in America. That is right here today.

We do not propose to divide it up equally. We do not propose a division of wealth, but we propose to limit poverty that we will allow to be inflicted upon any man's family. We will not say we are going to try to guarantee any equality, or $15,000 to families. No; but we do say that one third of the average is low enough for any one family to hold, that there should be a guaranty of a family wealth of around $5,000; enough for a home, and automobile, a radio, and the ordinary conveniences, and the opportunity to educate their children; a fair share of the income of this land thereafter to that family so there will be no such thing as merely the select to have those things, and so there will be no such thing as a family living in poverty and distress.

We have to limit fortunes. Our present plan is that we will allow no one man to own more than $50,000,000. We think that with that limit we will be able to carry out the balance of the program. It may be necessary that we limit it to less than $50,000,000. It may be necessary, in working out of the plans, that no man's fortune would be more than $10,000,000 or $15,000,000. But be that as it may, it will still be more than any one man, or any one man and his children and their children, will be able to spend in their lifetimes; and it is not necessary or reasonable to have wealth piled up beyond that point where we cannot prevent poverty among the masses.

Another thing we propose is old-age pension of $30 a month for everyone that is 60 years old. Now, we do not give this pension to a man making $1,000 a year, and we do not give it to him if he has $10,000 in property, but outside of that we do.

We will limit hours of work. There is not any necessity of having over-production. I think all you have got to do, ladies and gentlemen, is just limit the hours of work to such an extent as people will work only so long as is necessary to produce enough for all of the people to have what they need. Why, ladies and gentleman, let us say that all of these labor-saving devices reduce hours down to where you do not have to work but four hours a day; that is enough for these people, and then praise be the name of the Lord, if it gets that good. Let it be good and not a curse, and then we will have five hours a day and five days a week, or even less than that, and we might give a man a whole month off during a year, or give him two months; and we might do what other countries have seen fit to do, and what I did in Louisiana, by having schools by which adults could go back and learn the things that have been discovered since they went to school. . . .

Those are the things we propose to do. "Every man a king." Every man to eat when there is something to eat; all to wear something when there is something to wear. That makes us all sovereign. . . .

Chapter 18

"A THIRD OF THE NATION"

FRANKLIN D. ROOSEVELT'S SECOND INAUGURAL ADDRESS, JANUARY 20, 1937

Franklin Roosevelt was re-elected with ease in 1936, but the Great Depression lingered. Unemployment was reduced from 25 percent in 1933 to 14 percent as FDR took the oath of office for the second time. So, while the nation had recovered somewhat, and while FDR and the New Deal were able to instill some degree of confidence among the American people, the crisis was not nearly over. In his Second Inaugural Address, Roosevelt made it clear that there was much more work to be done. Although he took note of the improving economy, he made a point of telling his fellow Americans that he saw a country that still suffered tremendous hardships. This speech sought to dispel the notion that prosperity was around the corner. Rather, FDR sought to remind his fellow citizens that recovery remained incomplete, and that only renewed effort could restore the nation's fortunes.

Our progress out of the depression is obvious. But that is not all that you and I mean by the new order of things. Our pledge was not merely to do a patchwork job with secondhand materials. By using the new materials of social justice we have undertaken to erect on the old foundations a more enduring structure for the better use of future generations.

In that purpose we have been helped by achievements of mind and spirit. Old truths have been relearned; untruths have been unlearned. We have always known that heedless self-interest was bad morals; we know now that it is bad economics. Out of the collapse of a prosperity whose builders boasted their practicality has come the conviction that in the long run economic morality pays. We are beginning to wipe out the line that divides the practical from the ideal; and in so doing we are fashioning an instrument of unimagined power for the establishment of a morally better world.

This new understanding undermines the old admiration of worldly success as such. We are beginning to abandon our tolerance of the abuse of power by those who betray for profit the elementary decencies of life.

In this process evil things formerly accepted will not be so easily condoned. Hard-headedness will not so easily excuse hardheartedness. We are moving toward an era of good feeling. But we realize that there can be no era of good feeling save among men of good will.

For these reasons I am justified in believing that the greatest change we have witnessed has been the change in the moral climate of America.

Among men of good will, science and democracy together offer an ever-richer life and ever-larger satisfaction to the individual. With this change in our moral climate and our rediscovered ability to improve our economic order, we have set our feet upon the road of enduring progress.

Shall we pause now and turn our back upon the road that lies ahead? Shall we call this the promised land? Or, shall we continue on our way? For "each age is a dream that is dying, or one that is coming to birth."

Many voices are heard as we face a great decision. Comfort says, "Tarry a while." Opportunism says, "This is a good spot." Timidity asks, "How difficult is the road ahead?"

True, we have come far from the days of stagnation and despair. Vitality has been preserved. Courage and confidence have been restored. Mental and moral horizons have been extended.

But our present gains were won under the pressure of more than ordinary circumstances. Advance became imperative under the goad of fear and suffering. The times were on the side of progress.

To hold to progress today, however, is more difficult. Dulled conscience, irresponsibility, and ruthless self-interest already reappear. Such symptoms of prosperity may become portents of disaster! Prosperity already tests the persistence of our progressive purpose.

Let us ask again: Have we reached the goal of our vision of that fourth day of March 1933? Have we found our happy valley?

I see a great nation, upon a great continent, blessed with a great wealth of natural resources. Its hundred and thirty million people are at peace among themselves; they are making their country a good neighbor among the nations. I see a United States which can demonstrate that, under democratic methods of government, national wealth can be translated into a spreading volume of human comforts hitherto unknown, and the lowest standard of living can be raised far above the level of mere subsistence.

But here is the challenge to our democracy: In this nation I see tens of millions of its citizens—a substantial part of its whole population—who at this very moment are denied the greater part of what the very lowest standards of today call the necessities of life.

I see millions of families trying to live on incomes so meager that the pall of family disaster hangs over them day by day.

I see millions whose daily lives in city and on farm continue under conditions labeled indecent by a so-called polite society half a century ago.

I see millions denied education, recreation, and the opportunity to better their lot and the lot of their children.

I see millions lacking the means to buy the products of farm and factory and by their poverty denying work and productiveness to many other millions.

I see one-third of a nation ill-housed, ill-clad, ill-nourished.

It is not in despair that I paint you that picture. I paint it for you in hope—because the Nation, seeing and understanding the injustice in it, proposes to paint it out. We are determined to make every American citizen the subject of his country's interest and concern; and we will never regard any faithful law-abiding group within our borders as superfluous. The test of our progress is not whether we add more to the abundance of those who have much; it is whether we provide enough for those who have too little. . . .

Today we reconsecrate our country to long-cherished ideals in a suddenly changed civilization. In every land there are always at work forces that drive men apart and forces that draw men together. In our personal ambitions we are individualists. But in our seeking for economic and political progress as a nation, we all go up, or else we all go down, as one people. . . .

Chapter 19

"FOUR ESSENTIAL HUMAN FREEDOMS"

FRANKLIN D. ROOSEVELT'S STATE OF
THE UNION MESSAGE TO CONGRESS,
JANUARY 6, 1941

☞ The world was at war again in early 1941, when President Roosevelt addressed a joint session of Congress to talk about America's role in the conflict overseas. The United States remained at peace, but through the summer and fall of 1940, as the British single-handedly resisted Nazi Germany, Roosevelt made it clear that Britain's fight was America's as well. After FDR won a historic third term in 1940, he prepared to move the country ever closer to Britain's side. In this speech, Roosevelt argued that the nation faced a crisis of unprecedented proportions as democracy came under challenge from totalitarian powers around the world. He was not yet prepared to ask Congress for a declaration of war, but in this speech, he outlined plans for greater military spending, and he enunciated four great principles that ought to guide human affairs in the war's aftermath. The "Four Freedoms" became a rallying cry for Americans both before and after the nation's entry into the war.

I suppose that every realist knows that the democratic way of life is at this moment being directly assailed in every part of the world—assailed either by arms or by secret spreading of poisonous propaganda by those who seek to destroy unity and promote discord in nations that are still at peace.

During sixteen long months this assault has blotted out the whole pattern of democratic life in an appalling number of independent nations, great and small. And the assailants are still on the march, threatening other nations, great and small.

Therefore, as your President, performing my constitutional duty to "give to the Congress information of the state of the union," I find it unhappily necessary to report that the future and the safety of our country and of our democracy are overwhelmingly involved in events far beyond our borders.

Armed defense of democratic existence is now being gallantly waged in four continents. If that defense fails, all the population and all the resources of Europe and Asia, Africa and Australia will be dominated by conquerors. And let us remember that the total of those populations in those four continents, the total of those populations and their resources greatly exceeds the sum total of the population and the resources of the whole of the Western Hemisphere—yes, many times over.

In times like these it is immature—and, incidentally, untrue—for anybody to brag that an unprepared America, single-handed and with one hand tied behind its back, can hold off the whole world. No realistic American can expect from a dictator's peace international generosity, or return of true independence, or world disarmament, or freedom of expression, or freedom of religion—or even good business. Such a peace would bring no security for us or for our neighbors. Those who would give up essential liberty to purchase a little temporary safety deserve neither liberty nor safety. . . .

Certainly this is no time for any of us to stop thinking about the social and economic problems which are the root cause of the social revolution which is today a supreme factor in the world. For there is nothing mysterious about the foundations of a healthy and strong democracy. . . .

In the future days which we seek to make secure, we look forward to a world founded upon four essential human freedoms.

The first is freedom of speech and expression—everywhere in the world.

The second is freedom of every person to worship God in his own way—everywhere in the world.

The third is freedom from want, which, translated into world terms, means economic understandings which will secure to every nation a healthy peacetime life for its inhabitants—everywhere in the world.

The fourth is freedom from fear, which, translated into world terms, means a world-wide reduction of armaments to such a point and in such a thorough fashion that no nation will be in a position to commit an act of physical aggression against any neighbor—anywhere in the world.

That is no vision of a distant millennium. It is a definite basis for a kind of world attainable in our own time and generation. That kind of world is the very antithesis of the so-called "new order" of tyranny which the dictators seek to create with the crash of a bomb.

To that new order we oppose the greater conception—the moral order. A good society is able to face schemes of world domination and foreign revolutions alike without fear.

Since the beginning of our American history we have been engaged in change, in a perpetual, peaceful revolution, a revolution which goes on steadily, quietly, adjusting itself to changing conditions without the concentration camp or the quicklime in the ditch. The world order which we seek is the cooperation of free countries, working together in a friendly, civilized society.

This nation has placed its destiny in the hands, heads and hearts of its millions of free men and women, and its faith in freedom under the guidance of God. Freedom means the supremacy of human rights everywhere.

Our support goes to those who struggle to gain those rights and keep them. Our strength is our unity of purpose.

To that high concept there can be no end save victory.

Chapter 20

"A DATE WHICH WILL
LIVE IN INFAMY"

FRANKLIN D. ROOSEVELT'S
WAR MESSAGE TO CONGRESS,
DECEMBER 8, 1941

World War II arrived on American soil on December 7, 1941, when the Japanese attacked a U.S. naval base in Pearl Harbor, Hawaii. President Roosevelt, who had dropped any pretense of neutrality in 1941 by pushing Congress to approve aid to beleaguered Great Britain, addressed a joint session of Congress the following day, December 8. In somber tones, he emphasized that the Japanese attack was carried out under the cover of peace, while negotiations were underway between Washington and Tokyo. Shocked members of Congress needed no convincing. They quickly approved FDR's request for a declaration of war against Japan.

Yesterday, December 7, 1941—a date which will live in infamy—the United States of America was suddenly and deliberately attacked by naval and air forces of the Empire of Japan.

The United States was at peace with that nation and, at the solicitation of Japan, was still in conversation with its Government and its Emperor looking toward the maintenance of peace in the Pacific.

Indeed, one hour after Japanese air squadrons had commenced bombing Oahu, the Japanese Ambassador to the United States and his colleague delivered to the Secretary of State a formal reply to a recent American message. While this reply stated that it seemed useless to continue the existing diplomatic negotiations, it contained no threat or hint of war or armed attack.

It will be recorded that the distance of Hawaii from Japan makes it obvious that the attack was deliberately planned many days or even weeks ago. During the intervening time, the Japanese Government has deliberately sought to deceive the United States by false statements and expressions of hope for continued peace. The attack yesterday on the Hawaiian Islands has caused severe damage to American naval and military forces. Very many American lives have been lost. In addition, American ships have been reported torpedoed on the high seas between San Francisco and Honolulu.

Yesterday the Japanese Government also launched an attack against Malaya.

Last night Japanese forces attacked Hong Kong.

Last night Japanese forces attacked Guam.

Last night Japanese forces attacked the Philippine Islands.

Last night the Japanese attacked Wake Island.

This morning the Japanese attacked Midway Island.

Japan has, therefore, undertaken a surprise offensive extending throughout the Pacific area. The facts of yesterday speak for themselves. The people of the United States have already formed their opinions and well understand the implications to the very life and safety of our nation.

As Commander in Chief of the army and navy I have directed that all measures be taken for our defense.

Always will we remember the character of the onslaught against us.

No matter how long it may take us to overcome this premeditated invasion, the American people in their righteous might will win through to absolute victory. I believe I interpret the will of the Congress and of the people when I assert that we will not only defend ourselves to the uttermost but will make very certain that this form of treachery shall never endanger us again.

Hostilities exist. There is no blinking at the fact that our people, our territory and our interests are in grave danger.

With confidence in our armed forces—with the unbounding determination of our people—we will gain the inevitable triumph, so help us God.

I ask that the Congress declare that since the unprovoked and dastardly attack by Japan on Sunday, December 7, a state of war has existed between the United States and the Japanese Empire.

Chapter 21
"EVERY NATION MUST CHOOSE"

HARRY TRUMAN ANNOUNCES THE "TRUMAN DOCTRINE," MARCH 12, 1947

🎼☞ The Allied victory in World War II quickly gave way to recriminations and distrust between the West and the Soviet Union. Harry Truman, who became President after the death of Franklin Roosevelt in 1945, became disillusioned with Soviet actions in eastern and southern Europe. With communist insurgencies threatening Turkey and Greece in early 1947, Truman asked Congress for millions of dollars in aid for the two struggling regimes. But, in this speech, Truman also announced that the United States would unswervingly support other regimes engaged in similar struggles against Soviet-inspired communism. This policy became known as the Truman Doctrine.

The peoples of a number of countries of the world have recently had totalitarian regimes forced upon them against their will. The Government of the United States has made frequent protests against coercion and intimidation in violation of the Yalta agreement, in Poland, Rumania, and Bulgaria. I must also state that in a number of other countries there have been similar developments.

At the present moment in world history nearly every nation must choose between alternative ways of life. The choice is too often not a free one.

One way of life is based upon the will of the majority, and is distinguished by free institutions, representative government, free elections, guarantees of individual liberty, freedom of speech and religion, and freedom from political oppression.

The second way of life is based upon the will of a minority forcibly imposed upon the majority. It relies upon terror and oppression, a controlled press and radio, fixed elections, and the suppression of personal freedoms.

I believe that it must be the policy of the United States to support free peoples who are resisting attempted subjugation by armed minorities or by outside pressures. I believe that we must assist free peoples to work out their own destinies in their own way. I believe that our help should be primarily through economic and financial aid which is essential to economic stability and orderly political processes.

The world is not static, and the status quo is not sacred. But we cannot allow changes in the status quo in violation of the Charter of the United Nations by such methods as coercion, or by such subterfuges as political infiltration. In helping free and independent nations to maintain their freedom, the United States will be giving effect to the principles of the Charter of the United Nations.

It is necessary only to glance at a map to realize that the survival and integrity of the Greek nation are of grave importance in a much wider situation. If Greece should fall under the control of an armed minority, the effect upon its neighbor, Turkey, would be immediate and serious. Confusion and disorder might well spread throughout the entire Middle East. . . .

Should we fail to aid Greece and Turkey in this fateful hour, the effect will be far-reaching to the West as well as to the East. We must take immediate and resolute action. . . .

The seeds of totalitarian regimes are nurtured by misery and want. They spread and grow in the evil soil of poverty and strife. They reach their full growth when the hope of a people for a better life has died. We must keep that hope alive.

The free peoples of the world look to us for support in maintaining their freedoms. If we falter in our leadership, we may endanger the peace of the world and we shall surely endanger the welfare of our own nation.

Great responsibilities have been placed upon us by the swift movement of events. I am confident that the Congress will face these responsibilities squarely.

Chapter 22

"I SPEAK AS AN AMERICAN"

MARGARET CHASE SMITH'S DECLARATION OF CONSCIENCE, JUNE 1, 1950

In early 1950, Senator Joseph McCarthy of Wisconsin shocked the nation with a speech in Wheeling, West Virginia, during which he asserted that he had a list of known communists working in the U.S. State Department. The accusation came at a time of great anxiety in the United States over communist gains around the world. McCarthy's charges worsened fears that communism was winning the Cold War. But as McCarthy's recklessness grew, his Republican colleague from Maine, Margaret Chase Smith, delivered a powerful speech which, like Senator Robert La Follette a generation earlier, defended the right to dissent and to hold unfashionable beliefs. Smith never mentioned McCarthy and his smear tactics, but it was clear who her target was. Six other Republicans signed Smith's "Declaration of Conscience," an informal rebuke to McCarthy from within his own party.

I would like to speak briefly and simply about a serious national condition. It is a national feeling of fear and frustration that could result in national suicide and the end of everything that we Americans hold dear. . . .

I speak as a Republican. I speak as a woman. I speak as a United States Senator. I speak as an American.

The United States Senate has long enjoyed worldwide respect as the greatest deliberative body in the world. But recently that deliberative character has too often been debased to the level of a forum of hate and character assassination sheltered by the shield of congressional immunity. . . .

I think that it is high time for the United States Senate and its members to do some soul-searching—for us to weigh our consciences—on the manner in which we are performing our duty to the people of America—on the manner in which we are using or abusing our individual powers and privileges.

I think that it is high time that we remembered that we have sworn to uphold and defend the Constitution. I think that it is high time that we remembered that the Constitution, as amended, speaks not only of the freedom of speech but also of trial by jury instead of trial by accusation.

Whether it be a criminal prosecution in court or a character prosecution in the Senate, there is little practical distinction when the life of a person has been ruined.

Those of us who shout the loudest about Americanism in making character assassinations are all too frequently those who, by our own words and acts, ignore some of the basic principles of Americanism:

The right to criticize;

The right to hold unpopular beliefs;

The right to protest;

The right of independent thought.

The exercise of these rights should not cost one single American citizen his reputation or his right to a livelihood nor should he be in danger of losing his reputation or livelihood merely because he happens to know someone who holds unpopular beliefs. Who of us doesn't? Otherwise none of us could call our souls our own. Otherwise thought control would have set in.

The American people are sick and tired of being afraid to speak their minds lest they be politically smeared as "Communists" or "Fascists" by their opponents. Freedom of speech is not what it used to be in America. It has been so abused by some that it is not exercised by others. . . .

Today our country is being psychologically divided by the confusion and the suspicions that are bred in the United States Senate to spread like cancerous tentacles of "know nothing, suspect everything" attitudes. Today we have a Democratic Administration that has developed a mania for loose spending and loose programs. History is repeating itself—and the Republican Party again has the opportunity to emerge as the champion of unity and prudence. . . .

Surely these are sufficient reasons to make it clear to the American people that it is time for a change and that a Republican victory is necessary to the security of this country. Surely it is clear that this nation will continue to suffer as long as it is governed by the present ineffective Democratic Administration. . . .

Yet to displace it with a Republican regime embracing a philosophy that lacks political integrity or intellectual honesty would prove equally disastrous to this nation. The nation sorely needs a Republican victory.

But I don't want to see the Republican Party ride to political victory on the Four Horsemen of Calumny—Fear, Ignorance, Bigotry, and Smear.

I doubt if the Republican Party could—simply because I don't believe the American people will uphold any political party that puts political exploitation above national interest. Surely we Republicans aren't that desperate for victory.

I don't want to see the Republican Party win that way. While it might be a fleeting victory for the Republican Party, it would be a more lasting defeat for the American people. Surely it would ultimately be suicide for the Republican Party and the two-party system that has protected our American liberties from the dictatorship of a one party system. . . .

As a woman, I wonder how the mothers, wives, sisters, and daughters feel about the way in which members of their families have been politically mangled in the Senate debate—and I use the word "debate" advisedly.

As a United States Senator, I am not proud of the way in which the Senate has been made a publicity platform for irresponsible sensationalism. I am not proud of the reckless abandon in which unproved charges have been hurled from the side of the aisle. I am not proud of the obviously staged, undignified countercharges that have been attempted in retaliation from the other side of the aisle.

I don't like the way the Senate has been made a rendezvous for vilification, for selfish political gain at the sacrifice of individual reputations and national unity. I am not proud of the way we smear outsiders from the Floor of the Senate and hide behind the cloak of congressional immunity and still place ourselves beyond criticism on the Floor of the Senate.

As an American, I am shocked at the way Republicans and Democrats alike are playing directly into the Communist design of "confuse, divide, and conquer." As an American, I don't want a Democratic Administration "whitewash" or "cover-up" any more than I want a Republican smear or witch hunt.

As an American, I condemn a Republican "Fascist" just as much I condemn a Democratic "Communist." I condemn a Democrat "Fascist" just as much as I condemn a Republican "Communist." They are equally dangerous to you and me and to our country. As an American, I want to see our nation recapture the strength and unity it once had when we fought the enemy instead of ourselves. . . .

Chapter 23

"THE MILITARY-
INDUSTRIAL
COMPLEX"

**DWIGHT D. EISENHOWER'S FAREWELL
ADDRESS AS PRESIDENT,
JANUARY 17, 1961**

☞ Not all Presidents deliver farewell addresses before they leave office. Dwight Eisenhower chose to do so three days before his second term expired in 1961. The speech became perhaps the most famous valedictory in American presidential history, thanks to a single, memorable phrase: "The military-industrial complex." A career soldier and genuine war hero before becoming President in 1953, Eisenhower had the knowledge and credibility to warn Americans of the dangers he saw in an immensely profitable alliance between the military and defense contractors. Eisenhower did not deny the need for a stout defense in the nuclear age, but he did see danger in the growing influence of the military as well as the armaments industry. It was, he noted, something without precedent in U.S. history.

Three days from now, after a half century of service of our country, I shall lay down the responsibilities of office as, in traditional and solemn ceremony, the authority of the Presidency is vested in my successor.

This evening I come to you with a message of leave-taking and farewell, and to share a few final thoughts with you, my countrymen. . . .

We now stand ten years past the midpoint of a century that has witnessed four major wars among great nations. Three of these involved our own country. Despite these holocausts America is today the strongest, the most influential and most productive nation in the world. Understandably proud of this pre-eminence, we yet realize that America's leadership and prestige depend, not merely upon our unmatched material progress, riches and military strength, but on how we use our power in the interests of world peace and human betterment. . . .

The record of many decades stands as proof that our people and their Government have, in the main, understood these truths and have responded to them well in the face of stress and threat. But threats, new in kind or degree, constantly arise. I mention two only.

A vital element in keeping the peace is our military establishment. Our arms must be mighty, ready for instant action, so that no potential aggressor may be tempted to risk his own destruction.

Our military organization today bears little relation to that known by any of my predecessors in peacetime, or indeed by the fighting men of World War II or Korea.

Until the latest of our world conflicts, the United States had no armaments industry. American makers of plowshares could, with time and as required, make swords as well. But now we can no longer risk emergency improvisation of national defense; we have been compelled to create a permanent armaments industry of vast proportions. Added to this, three and a half million men and women are directly engaged in the defense establishment. We annually spend on military security more than the net income of all United States corporations.

This conjunction of an immense military establishment and a large arms industry is new in the American experience. The total influence—economic, political, even spiritual—is felt in every city, every State house, every office of the Federal government. We recognize the imperative need for this development. Yet we must not fail to comprehend its grave implications. Our toil, resources and livelihood are all involved; so is the very structure of our society.

In the councils of government, we must guard against the acquisition of unwarranted influence, whether sought or unsought, by the military-industrial complex. The potential for the disastrous rise of misplaced power exists and will persist.

We must never let the weight of this combination endanger our liberties or democratic processes. We should take nothing for granted. Only an alert and knowledgeable citizenry can compel the proper meshing of the huge industrial and military machinery of defense with our peaceful methods and goals, so that security and liberty may prosper together.

Akin to, and largely responsible for the sweeping changes in our industrial-military posture, has been the technological revolution during recent decades.

In this revolution, research has become central; it also becomes more formalized, complex, and costly. A steadily increasing share is conducted for, by, or at the direction of, the Federal government.

Today, the solitary inventor, tinkering in his shop, has been overshadowed by task forces of scientists in laboratories and testing fields. In the same fashion, the free university, historically the fountainhead of free ideas and scientific discovery, has experienced a revolution in the conduct of research. Partly because of the huge costs involved, a government contract becomes virtually a substitute for intellectual curiosity. For every old blackboard there are now hundreds of new electronic computers.

The prospect of domination of the nation's scholars by Federal employment, project allocations, and the power of money is ever present—and is gravely to be regarded.

Yet, in holding scientific research and discovery in respect, as we should, we must also be alert to the equal and opposite danger that public policy could itself become the captive of a scientific-technological elite.

It is the task of statesmanship to mold, to balance, and to integrate these and other forces, new and old, within the principles of our democratic system—ever aiming toward the supreme goals of our free society. . . .

Chapter 24

"ASK NOT WHAT YOUR COUNTRY CAN DO FOR YOU"

JOHN F. KENNEDY'S INAUGURAL ADDRESS, JANUARY 20, 1961

☞ On a cold winter's day in Washington, D.C., the youngest person ever elected to the presidency took the oath of office and delivered one of the most memorable Inaugural Addresses in U.S. history. John F. Kennedy was the first President born in the twentieth century, and in his stirring speech, he declared that the torch of leadership had been passed to his generation—men and women who had lived through the Great Depression and World War II. The trumpet of leadership, Kennedy said, summoned Americans to defend freedom at a time of maximum peril. Confident as ever, Kennedy declared that he welcomed the opportunity to lead the nation and defend its values at the height of the Cold War with the Soviet Union. With its brilliant imagery and poetic cadence, John Kennedy's Inaugural Address is a masterpiece of American political oratory.

We observe today not a victory of party but a celebration of freedom—symbolizing an end as well as a beginning—signifying renewal as well as change. For I have sworn before you and Almighty God the same solemn oath our forebears prescribed nearly a century and three-quarters ago.

The world is very different now. For man holds in his mortal hands the power to abolish all forms of human poverty and all forms of human life. And yet the same revolutionary beliefs for which our forebears fought are still at issue around the globe—the belief that the rights of man come not from the generosity of the state but from the hand of God.

We dare not forget today that we are the heirs of that first revolution. Let the word go forth from this time and place, to friend and foe alike, that the torch has been passed to a new generation of Americans—born in this century, tempered by war, disciplined by a hard and bitter peace, proud of our ancient heritage—and unwilling to witness or permit the slow undoing of those human rights to which this nation has always been committed, and to which we are committed today at home and around the world.

Let every nation know, whether it wishes us well or ill, that we shall pay any price, bear any burden, meet any hardship, support any friend, oppose any foe to assure the survival and the success of liberty. This much we pledge—and more.

To those old allies whose cultural and spiritual origins we share, we pledge the loyalty of faithful friends. United, there is little we cannot do in a host of cooperative ventures. Divided, there is little we can do—for we dare not meet a powerful challenge at odds and split asunder.

To those new states whom we welcome to the ranks of the free, we pledge our word that one form of colonial control shall not have passed away merely to be replaced by a far more iron tyranny. We shall not always expect to find them supporting our view. But we shall always hope to find them strongly supporting their own freedom—and to remember that, in the past, those who foolishly sought power by riding the back of the tiger ended up inside.

To those people in the huts and villages of half the globe struggling to break the bonds of mass misery, we pledge our best efforts to help them help themselves, for whatever period is required—not because the Communists may be doing it, not because we seek their votes, but because it is right. If a free society cannot help the many who are poor, it cannot save the few who are rich. . . .

Finally, to those nations who would make themselves our adversary, we offer not a pledge but a request: that both sides begin anew the quest for peace, before the dark powers of destruction unleashed by science engulf all humanity in planned or accidental self-destruction.

We dare not tempt them with weakness. For only when our arms are sufficient beyond doubt can we be certain beyond doubt that they will never be employed. But neither can two great and powerful groups of nations take comfort from our present course—both sides overburdened by the cost of modern weapons, both rightly alarmed by the steady spread of the deadly atom, yet both racing to alter that uncertain balance of terror that stays the hand of mankind's final war. So let us begin anew—remembering on both sides that civility is not a sign of weakness, and sincerity is always subject to proof. Let us never negotiate out of fear. But let us never fear to negotiate.

Let both sides explore what problems unite us instead of belaboring those problems which divide us.

Let both sides, for the first time, formulate serious and precise proposals for the inspection and control of arms—and bring the absolute power to destroy other nations under the absolute control of all nations.

Let both sides seek to invoke the wonders of science instead of its terror. Together let us explore the stars, conquer the deserts, eradicate disease, tap the ocean depths and encourage the arts and commerce.

Let both sides unite to heed in all corners of the earth the command of Isaiah—to "undo the heavy burdens . . . [and] let the oppressed go free."

And if a beachhead of cooperation may push back the jungle of suspicion, let both sides join in creating a new endeavor not a new balance of power, but a new world of law, where the strong are just and the weak secure and the peace preserved. All this will not be finished in the first 100 days. Nor will it be finished in the first 1,000 days, not in the life of this Administration, nor even perhaps in our lifetime on this planet. But let us begin.

In your hands, my fellow citizens, more than mine, will rest the final success or failure of our course. Since this country was founded, each generation of Americans has been summoned to give testimony to its national loyalty. The graves of young Americans who answered the call to service surround the globe.

Now the trumpet summons us again—not as a call to bear arms, though arms we need—not as a call to battle, though embattled we are—but a call to bear the burden of a long twilight struggle year in and year out, "rejoicing in hope, patient in tribulation"—a struggle against the common enemies of man: tyranny, poverty, disease and war itself. . . .

In the long history of the world, only a few generations have been granted the role of defending freedom in its hour of maximum danger. I do not shrink from this responsibility—I welcome it. I do not believe that any of us would exchange places with any other people or any other generation. The energy, the faith, the devotion which we bring to this endeavor will light our country and all who serve it—and the glow from that fire can truly light the world.

And so, my fellow Americans: ask not what your country can do for you—ask what you can do for your country.

My fellow citizens of the world: ask not what America will do for you, but what together we can do for the freedom of man.

Finally, whether you are citizens of America or citizens of the world, ask of us here the same high standards of strength and sacrifice which we ask of you. With a good conscience our only sure reward, with history the final judge of our deeds, let us go forth to lead the land we love, asking His blessing and His help, but knowing that here on earth God's work must truly be our own.

Chapter 25

"THE PURSUIT OF DISARMAMENT"

JOHN F. KENNEDY'S PEACE SPEECH AT AMERICAN UNIVERSITY, JUNE 10, 1963

☞ The Cold War became uncomfortably warm in late October 1962, when the Kennedy administration declared that it would not accept the existence of nuclear missiles on the island of Cuba. The Soviet Union chose to back down rather than continue to attempt to deploy the weapons in Cuba, but for several days, the United States and the Soviets were close to outright war. The Cuban Missile Crisis led President Kennedy, an ardent Cold Warrior, to reconsider his views about the U.S.– Soviet conflict. In his speech, little noticed at the time, Kennedy asked his fellow citizens to join him in a reconsideration of their attitudes toward peace, the Cold War, and the Russian people. Some historians consider this speech to be Kennedy's greatest.

Some say that it is useless to speak of world peace or world law or world disarmament—and that it will be useless until the leaders of the Soviet Union adopt a more enlightened attitude. I hope they do. I believe we can help them do it. But I also believe that we must reexamine our own attitude—as individuals and as a Nation—for our attitude is as essential as theirs. And every graduate of this school, every thoughtful citizen who despairs of war and wishes to bring peace, should begin by looking inward—by examining his own attitude toward the possibilities of peace, toward the Soviet Union, toward the course of the cold war and toward freedom and peace here at home.

First: Let us examine our attitude toward peace itself. Too many of us think it is impossible. Too many think it unreal. But that is a dangerous, defeatist belief. It leads to the conclusion that war is inevitable—that mankind is doomed—that we are gripped by forces we cannot control.

We need not accept that view. Our problems are manmade—therefore, they can be solved by man. And man can be as big as he wants. No problem of human destiny is beyond human beings. Man's reason and spirit have often solved the seemingly unsolvable—and we believe they can do it again. . . .

Second: Let us reexamine our attitude toward the Soviet Union. . . . No government or social system is so evil that its people must be considered as lacking in virtue. As Americans, we find communism profoundly repugnant as a negation of personal freedom and dignity. But we can still hail the Russian people for their many achievements—in science and space, in economic and industrial growth, in culture and in acts of courage.

Among the many traits the peoples of our two countries have in common, none is stronger than our mutual abhorrence of war. Almost unique, among the major world powers, we have never been at war with each other. And no nation in the history of battle ever suffered more than the Soviet Union suffered in the course of the Second World War. At least twenty million lost their lives. Countless millions of homes and farms were burned or sacked. A third of the nation's territory, including nearly two thirds of its industrial base, was turned into a wasteland—a loss equivalent to the devastation of this country east of Chicago. . . .

Third: Let us reexamine our attitude toward the Cold War, remembering that we are not engaged in a debate, seeking to pile up debating points. We are not here distributing blame or pointing the finger of judgment. We must deal with the world as it is, and not as it might have been had the history of the last 18 years been different.

We must, therefore, persevere in the search for peace in the hope that constructive changes within the Communist bloc might bring within reach solutions which now seem beyond us. We must conduct our affairs in such a way that it becomes in the Communist's interest to agree on a genuine peace. Above all, while defending our own vital interests, nuclear powers must avert those confrontations which bring an adversary to a choice of either a humiliating retreat or a nuclear war. To adopt that kind of course in the nuclear age would be evidence only of the bankruptcy of our policy—or of a collective death-wish for the world. To secure these ends, America's weapons are nonprovocative, carefully controlled, designed to deter, and capable of selective use. Our military forces are committed to peace and disciplined in self-restraint. Our diplomats are instructed to avoid unnecessary irritants and purely rhetorical hostility. . . .

The pursuit of disarmament has been an effort of

this Government since the 1920s. It has been urgently sought by the past three administrations. And however dim the prospects may be today, we intend to continue this effort to continue it in order that all countries, including our own, can better grasp what the problems and possibilities of disarmament are.

The one major area of these negotiations where the end is in sight, yet where a fresh start is badly needed, is in a treaty to outlaw nuclear tests. The conclusion of such a treaty, so near and yet so far, would check the spiraling arms race in one of its most dangerous areas. It would place the nuclear powers in a position to deal more effectively with one of the greatest hazards which man faces in 1963, the further spread of nuclear arms. It would increase our security—it would decrease the prospects of war. Surely this goal is sufficiently important to require our steady pursuit, yielding neither to the temptation to give up the whole effort nor the temptation to give up our insistence on vital and responsible safeguards. I am taking this opportunity, therefore, to announce two important decisions in this regard.

First: Chairman Khrushchev, Prime Minister Macmillan, and I have agreed that high-level discussions will shortly begin in Moscow looking toward early agreement on a comprehensive test ban treaty. Our hopes must be tempered with the caution of history but with our hopes go the hopes of all mankind.

Second: To make clear our good faith and solemn convictions on the matter, I now declare that the United States does not propose to conduct nuclear tests in the atmosphere so long as other states do not do so. We will not be the first to resume. Such a declaration is no substitute for a formal binding treaty, but I hope it will help us achieve one. Nor would such a treaty be a substitute for disarmament, but I hope it will help us achieve it.

Finally, my fellow Americans, let us examine our attitude toward peace and freedom here at home. The quality and spirit of our own society must justify and support our efforts abroad. We must show it in the dedication of our own lives—as many of you who are graduating today will have a unique opportunity to do, by serving without pay in the Peace Corps abroad or in the proposed National Service Corps here at home.

But wherever we are, we must all, in our daily lives, live up to the age-old faith that peace and freedom walk together. . . .

Chapter 26

"A MORAL ISSUE"

JOHN F. KENNEDY'S
CIVIL RIGHTS MESSAGE,
JUNE 11, 1963

🖙 The early 1960s saw open conflict in the nation's South as courageous African Americans demanded an end to legal segregation, state-sanctioned repression, and overt discrimination. The Kennedy administration, focused relentlessly on foreign affairs, was caught unprepared for this powerful grassroots movement. In the spring of 1963, however, President Kennedy responded forcefully when Alabama Governor George Wallace resisted federal efforts to desegregate the University of Alabama, a public institution. On the evening of June 11—a day after his speech at American University—President Kennedy delivered a nationally televised address in which he declared that the African-American demands for equality were not a sectional issue, and not even a legal issue, but a moral issue. Kennedy was late in raising his voice on behalf of the civil rights movement, but the language in this speech left little doubt about his views.

This afternoon, following a series of threats and defiant statements, the presence of Alabama National Guardsmen was required on the University of Alabama to carry out the final and unequivocal order of the United States District Court of the Northern District of Alabama. That order called for the admission of two clearly qualified young Alabama residents who happened to have been born Negro.

That they were admitted peacefully on the campus is due in good measure to the conduct of the students of the University of Alabama, who met their responsibilities in a constructive way.

I hope that every American, regardless of where he lives, will stop and examine his conscience about this and other related incidents. This Nation was founded by men of many nations and backgrounds. It was founded on the principle that all men are created equal, and that the rights of every man are diminished when the rights of one man are threatened.

Today we are committed to a worldwide struggle to promote and protect the rights of all who wish to be free. And when Americans are sent to Vietnam or West Berlin, we do not ask for whites only. It ought to be possible, therefore, for American students of any color to attend any public institution they select without having to be backed up by troops.

It ought to be possible for American consumers of any color to receive equal service in places of public accommodation, such as hotels and restaurants and theaters and retail stores, without being forced to resort to demonstrations in the street, and it ought to be possible for American citizens of any color to register and to vote in a free election without interference or fear of reprisal.

It ought to be possible, in short, for every American to enjoy the privileges of being American without regard to his race or his color. In short, every American ought to have the right to be treated as he would wish to be treated, as one would wish his children to be treated. But this is not the case.

The Negro baby born in America today, regardless of the section of the Nation in which he is born, has about one-half as much chance of completing high school as a white baby born in the same place on the same day, one-third as much chance of completing college, one-third as much chance of becoming a professional man, twice as much chance of becoming unemployed, about one-seventh as much chance of earning $10,000 a year, a life expectancy which is seven years shorter, and the prospects of earning only half as much.

This is not a sectional issue. Difficulties over segregation and discrimination exist in every city, in every State of the Union, producing in many cities a rising tide of discontent that threatens the public safety. Nor is this a partisan issue. In a time of domestic crisis men of good will and generosity should be able to unite regardless of party or politics. This is not even a legal or legislative issue alone. It is better to settle these matters in the courts than on the streets, and new laws are needed at every level, but law alone cannot make men see right.

We are confronted primarily with a moral issue. It is as old as the scriptures and is as clear as the American Constitution.

The heart of the question is whether all Americans are to be afforded equal rights and equal opportunities, whether we are going to treat our fellow Americans as we want to be treated. If an American, because his skin is dark, cannot eat lunch in a restaurant open to the public, if he cannot send his children to the best public school available, if he cannot vote for the public officials who represent him, if, in short, he cannot enjoy the full and free life which all of us want, then who among us would be content to have the color of his skin changed and stand in his place?

Who among us would then be content with the counsels of patience and delay?

One hundred years of delay have passed since President Lincoln freed the slaves, yet their heirs, their grandsons, are not fully free. They are not yet freed from the bonds of injustice. They are not yet freed from social and economic oppression. And this Nation, for all its hopes and all its boasts, will not be fully free until all its citizens are free.

We preach freedom around the world, and we mean it, and we cherish our freedom here at home, but are we to say to the world, and much more importantly, to each other that this is a land of the free except for the Negroes; that we have no second-class citizens except Negroes; that we have no class or caste system, no ghettoes, no master race except with respect to Negroes?

Now the time has come for this Nation to fulfill its promise. The events in Birmingham and elsewhere have so increased the cries for equality that no city or State or legislative body can prudently choose to ignore them. . . .

We face, therefore, a moral crisis as a country and as a people. It cannot be met by repressive police action. It cannot be left to increased demonstrations in the streets. It cannot be quieted by token moves or talk. It is a time to act in the Congress, in your State and local legislative body and, above all, in all of our daily lives. It is not enough to pin the blame on others, to say this is a problem of one section of the country or another, or deplore the fact that we face. A great change is at hand, and our task, our obligation, is to make that revolution, that change, peaceful and constructive for all.

Those who do nothing are inviting shame as well as violence. Those who act boldly are recognizing right as well as reality. . . .

Chapter 27

"ICH BIN EIN BERLINER"

JOHN F. KENNEDY'S SPEECH AT THE BERLIN WALL, JUNE 26, 1963

☞ Slightly more than two weeks after President Kennedy asked the nation to reassess its view of the Cold War, Kennedy himself delivered one of the rawest, angriest, most passionate speeches of the Cold War era. It became a classic because of the emotion he expressed and because of the emotions he inspired among the hundreds of thousands of West Berliners who heard his defiant words. Kennedy used the Berlin Wall, constructed to prevent East Berliners from fleeing their communist-controlled portion of the city, as a symbol of the differences between the free world and the communist world. His use of the German phrase for "I am a Berliner," while perhaps not grammatically correct, thrilled his audience and retains its power a half-century later.

I am proud to come to this city as the guest of your distinguished Mayor, who has symbolized throughout the world the fighting spirit of West Berlin. And I am proud to visit the Federal Republic with your distinguished Chancellor who for so many years has committed Germany to democracy and freedom and progress, and to come here in the company of my fellow American, General Clay, who has been in this city during its great moments of crisis and will come again if ever needed.

Two thousand years ago the proudest boast was "civis Romanus sum." Today, in the world of freedom, the proudest boast is "Ich bin ein Berliner."

I appreciate my interpreter translating my German!

There are many people in the world who really don't understand, or say they don't, what is the great issue between the free world and the Communist world. Let them come to Berlin. There are some who say that communism is the wave of the future. Let them come to Berlin. And there are some who say in Europe and elsewhere we can work with the Communists. Let them come to Berlin. And there are even a few who say that it is true that communism is an evil system, but it permits us to make economic progress. Lass' sie nach Berlin kommen. Let them come to Berlin.

Freedom has many difficulties and democracy is not perfect, but we have never had to put a wall up to keep our people in, to prevent them from leaving us. I want to say, on behalf of my countrymen, who live many miles away on the other side of the Atlantic, who are far distant from you, that they take the greatest pride that they have been able to share with you, even from a distance, the story of the last 18 years. I know of no town, no city, that has been besieged for 18 years that still lives with the vitality and the force, and the hope and the determination of the city of West Berlin. While the wall is the most obvious and vivid demonstration of the failures of the Communist system, for all the world to see, we take no satisfaction in it, for it is, as your Mayor has said, an offense not only against history but an offense against humanity, separating families, dividing husbands and wives and brothers and sisters, and dividing a people who wish to be joined together.

What is true of this city is true of Germany—real, lasting peace in Europe can never be assured as long as one German out of four is denied the elementary right of free men, and that is to make a free choice. In 18 years of peace and good faith, this generation of Germans has earned the right to be free, including the right to unite their families and their nation in lasting peace, with good will to all people. You live in a defended island of freedom, but your life is part of the main. So let me ask you as I close, to lift your eyes beyond the dangers of today, to the hopes of tomorrow, beyond the freedom merely of this city of Berlin, or your country of Germany, to the advance of freedom everywhere, beyond the wall to the day of peace with justice, beyond yourselves and ourselves to all mankind.

Freedom is indivisible, and when one man is enslaved, all are not free. When all are free, then we can look forward to that day when this city will be joined as one and this country and this great Continent of Europe in a peaceful and hopeful globe. When that day finally comes, as it will, the people of West Berlin can take sober satisfaction in the fact that they were in the front lines for almost two decades.

All free men, wherever they may live, are citizens of Berlin, and, therefore, as a free man, I take pride in the words "Ich bin ein Berliner."

Chapter 28

"I HAVE A DREAM"

DR. MARTIN LUTHER KING, JR.'S SPEECH TO CIVIL RIGHTS MARCHERS IN WASHINGTON, AUGUST 28, 1963

☞ African-American demands for full equality and so-cial justice reached a climax on a summer's day in 1963 when Dr. Martin Luther King, Jr., winner of the Nobel Peace Prize, addressed some 250,000 demonstrators on the Mall in Washington. The huge gathering heard one of the most stirring speeches in American history, filled with memorable phrases and imagery. Dr. King's ca-dence and timing gave the speech even more power as he articulated the grievances and hopes of African Americans in the early 1960s. The speech lives on as a landmark in American political rhetoric and a testa-ment to the impact of words and ideas.

I am happy to join with you today in what will go down in history as the greatest demonstration for free-dom in the history of our nation.

Five score years ago, a great American in whose symbolic shadow we stand today signed the Emancipa-tion Proclamation. This momentous decree came as a great beacon light of hope to millions of Negro slaves who had been seared in the flames of withering injustice. It came as a joyous daybreak to end the long night of their captivity.

But one hundred years later, the Negro still is not free. One hundred years later, the life of the Negro is still sadly crippled by the manacles of segregation and the chains of discrimination. One hundred years later, the Negro lives on a lonely island of poverty in the midst of a vast ocean of material prosperity. One hundred years later, the Negro is still languished in the corners of American society and finds himself an exile in his own land. And so we've come here today to dramatize a shameful condition.

In a sense we've come to our nation's Capital to cash a check. When the architects of our republic wrote the magnificent words of the Constitution and the Declaration of Independence, they were signing a promissory note to which every American was to fall heir. This note was a promise that all men—yes, black men as well as white men—would be guaranteed the unalienable rights of life, liberty and the pursuit of happiness.

It is obvious today that America has defaulted on this promissory note insofar as her citizens of color are concerned. Instead of honoring this sacred obligation, America has given the Negro people a bad check, a check which has come back marked "insufficient funds."

But we refuse to believe that the bank of justice is bankrupt. We refuse to believe that there are insufficient funds in the great vaults of opportunity of this nation. And so we've come to cash this check, a check that will give us upon demand the riches of freedom and the security of justice.

We have also come to this hallowed spot to remind America of the fierce urgency of now. This is no time to engage in the luxury of cooling off or to take the tranquilizing drug of gradualism. Now is the time to make real the promises of democracy. Now is the time to rise from the dark and desolate valley of segregation to the sunlit path of racial justice. Now is the time to lift our nation from the quicksands of racial injustice to the solid rock of brotherhood. Now is the time to make justice a reality for all of God's children.

It would be fatal for the nation to overlook the urgency of the moment. This sweltering summer of the Negro's legitimate discontent will not pass until there is an invigorating autumn of freedom and equality. Nineteen sixty-three is not an end, but a beginning. Those who hope that the Negro needed to blow off steam and will now be content will have a rude awakening if the nation returns to business as usual. There will be neither rest nor tranquility in America until the Negro is granted his citizenship rights. The whirlwinds of revolt will continue to shake the foundations of our nation until the bright day of justice emerges.

But there is something that I must say to my people, who stand on the warm threshold which leads into the palace of justice: In the process of gaining our rightful place, we must not be guilty of wrongful deeds. Let us not seek to satisfy our thirst for freedom by drinking from the cup of bitterness and hatred. We must forever conduct our struggle on the high plane of dignity and discipline. We must not allow our creative protest to degenerate into physical violence. Again and again, we must rise to the majestic heights of meeting physical force with soul force.

The marvelous new militancy which has engulfed the Negro community must not lead us to a distrust of all white people, for many of our white brothers, as evidenced by their presence here today, have come to realize that their destiny is tied up with our destiny. And they have come to realize that their freedom is inextricably bound to our freedom. We cannot walk alone.

And as we walk, we must make the pledge that we shall always march ahead. We cannot turn back. There are those who are asking the devotees of civil rights, "When will you be satisfied?" We can never be satisfied as long as the Negro is the victim of the unspeakable horrors of police brutality. We can never be satisfied as long as our bodies, heavy with the fatigue of travel, cannot gain lodging in the motels of the highways and the hotels of the cities. We cannot be satisfied as long as the Negro's basic mobility is from a smaller ghetto to a larger one. We can never be satisfied as long as our children are stripped of their selfhood and robbed of their dignity by signs stating: "For Whites Only." We cannot be satisfied as long as a Negro in Mississippi cannot vote and a Negro in New York believes he has nothing for which to vote. No, no, we are not satisfied, and we will not be satisfied until "justice rolls down like waters, and righteousness like a mighty stream."

I am not unmindful that some of you have come here out of great trials and tribulations. Some of you have come fresh from narrow jail cells. And some of you have come from areas where your quest for freedom left you battered by the storms of persecution and staggered by the winds of police brutality. You have been the veterans of creative suffering. Continue to work with the faith that unearned suffering is redemptive.

Go back to Mississippi, go back to Alabama, go back to South Carolina, go back to Georgia, go back to Louisiana, go back to the slums and ghettos of our northern cities, knowing that somehow this situation can and will be changed. Let us not wallow in the valley of despair.

I say to you today, my friends, so even though we face the difficulties of today and tomorrow, I still have a dream. It is a dream deeply rooted in the American dream.

I have a dream that one day this nation will rise up and live out the true meaning of its creed: "We hold these truths to be self-evident, that all men are created equal."

I have a dream that one day on the red hills of Georgia, the sons of former slaves and the sons of former slave owners will be able to sit down together at the table of brotherhood.

I have a dream that one day even the state of Mississippi, a state sweltering with the heat of injustice, sweltering with the heat of oppression, will be transformed into an oasis of freedom and justice.

I have a dream that my four little children will one day live in a nation where they will not be judged by the color of their skin but by the content of their character. I have a dream today!

I have a dream that one day, down in Alabama—with its vicious racists, with its Governor having his lips dripping with the words of interposition and nullification—one day right there in Alabama little black boys and black girls will be able to join hands with little white boys and white girls as sisters and brothers. I have a dream today!

I have a dream that one day every valley shall be exalted, and every hill and mountain shall be made low, the rough places will be made plain, and the crooked places will be made straight; "and the glory of the Lord shall be revealed and all flesh shall see it together."

This is our hope. This is the faith that I go back to the South with. With this faith, we will be able to hew out of the mountain of despair a stone of hope. With this faith, we will be able to transform the jangling discords of our nation into a beautiful symphony of brotherhood. With this faith, we will be able to work together, to pray together, to struggle together, to go to jail together, to stand up for freedom together, knowing that we will be free one day.

This will be the day—this will be the day when all of God's children will be able to sing with new meaning: "My country 'tis of thee, sweet land of liberty, of thee I sing. Land where my fathers died, land of the Pilgrim's pride; from every mountainside, let freedom ring!" And if America is to be a great nation, this must become true.

And so let freedom ring from the prodigious hilltops of New Hampshire. Let freedom ring from the mighty mountains of New York. Let freedom ring from the heightening Alleghenies of Pennsylvania. Let freedom ring from the snow-capped Rockies of Colorado. Let freedom ring from the curvaceous slopes of California.

But not only that. Let freedom ring from Stone Mountain of Georgia. Let freedom ring from Lookout Mountain of Tennessee. Let freedom ring from every hill and molehill of Mississippi. "From every mountainside, let freedom ring."

And when this happens, when we allow freedom ring, when we let it ring from every village and every hamlet, from every state and every city, we will be able to speed up that day when *all* of God's children, black men and white men, Jews and Gentiles, Protestants and Catholics, will be able to join hands and sing in the words of the old Negro spiritual, "Free at last! Free at last! Thank *God* Almighty, we are free at last!"

Chapter 29
"WE SHALL OVERCOME"

LYNDON B. JOHNSON'S CIVIL RIGHTS SPEECH, MARCH 15, 1965

☞ Lyndon Johnson, the first Southern president since the Civil War, understood the historic importance of the civil rights movement, perhaps more profoundly than did his assassinated predecessor, John Kennedy. Johnson framed a new civil rights bill as a tribute to the fallen Kennedy in 1964, winning passage of a measure many Southern Democrats opposed. The following year, Johnson sought to build on the momentum for equality and justice by introducing a new voting rights act that would outlaw measures intended to make it more difficult for African Americans to exercise their hard-won franchise. Johnson delivered this speech to a joint session of Congress. His use of the phrase "we shall overcome" was a memorable tribute to the civil rights marchers for whom the song "We Shall Overcome" was an anthem.

I speak tonight for the dignity of man and the destiny of democracy.

I urge every member of both parties, Americans of

all religions and of all colors, from every section of this country, to join me in that cause.

At times history and fate meet at a single time in a single place to shape a turning point in man's unending search for freedom. So it was at Lexington and Concord. So it was a century ago at Appomattox. So it was last week in Selma, Alabama.

There, long-suffering men and women peacefully protested the denial of their rights as Americans. Many were brutally assaulted. One good man, a man of God, was killed.

There is no cause for pride in what has happened in Selma. There is no cause for self-satisfaction in the long denial of equal rights of millions of Americans. But there is cause for hope and for faith in our democracy in what is happening here tonight.

For the cries of pain and the hymns and protests of oppressed people have summoned into convocation all the majesty of this great Government—the Government of the greatest Nation on earth.

Our mission is at once the oldest and the most basic of this country: to right wrong, to do justice, to serve man.

In our time we have come to live with moments of great crisis. Our lives have been marked with debate about great issues; issues of war and peace, issues of prosperity and depression. But rarely in any time does an issue lay bare the secret heart of America itself.

Rarely are we met with a challenge, not to our growth or abundance, our welfare or our security, but rather to the values and the purposes and the meaning of our beloved Nation.

The issue of equal rights for American Negroes is such an issue. And should we defeat every enemy, should we double our wealth and conquer the stars, and still be unequal to this issue, then we will have failed as a people and as a nation.

There is no Negro problem. There is no Southern problem. There is no Northern problem. There is only an American problem. And we are met here tonight as Americans—not as Democrats or Republicans—we are met here as Americans to solve that problem.

This was the first nation in the history of the world to be founded with a purpose. The great phrases of that purpose still sound in every American heart, North and South: "All men are created equal"—"government by consent of the governed"—"give me liberty or give me death." Well, those are not just clever words, or those are not just empty theories. In their name Americans have fought and died for two centuries, and tonight around the world they stand there as guardians of our liberty, risking their lives.

Those words are a promise to every citizen that he shall share in the dignity of man. This dignity cannot be found in a man's possessions; it cannot be found in his power, or in his position. It really rests on his right to be treated as a man equal in opportunity to all others. It says that he shall share in freedom, he shall choose his leaders, educate his children, and provide for his family according to his ability and his merits as a human being.

To apply any other test—to deny a man his hopes because of his color or race, his religion or the place of his birth—is not only to do injustice, it is to deny America and to dishonor the dead who gave their lives for American freedom.

Our fathers believed that if this noble view of the rights of man was to flourish, it must be rooted in democracy. The most basic right of all was the right to choose your own leaders. The history of this country, in large measure, is the history of the expansion of that right to all of our people.

Many of the issues of civil rights are very complex and most difficult. But about this there can and should be no argument. Every American citizen must have an equal right to vote. There is no reason which can excuse the denial of that right. There is no duty which weighs more heavily on us than the duty we have to ensure that right.

Yet the harsh reality is that in many places in this country men and women are kept from voting simply because they are Negroes.

Every device of which human ingenuity is capable has been used to deny this right. The Negro citizen may go to register only to be told that the day is wrong, or the hour is late, or the official in charge is absent And if he persists, and if he manages to present himself to the registrar, he may be disqualified because he did not spell out his middle name or because he abbreviated a word on the application. And if he manages to fill out an application he is given a test. The registrar is the sole judge of whether he passes this test. He may be asked to recite the entire Constitution, or explain the most complex provisions of State law. And even a college degree cannot be used to prove that he can read and write.

For the fact is that the only way to pass these barriers is to show a white skin. Experience has clearly shown that the existing process of law cannot overcome systematic and ingenious discrimination. No law that we now have on the books—and I have helped to put three of them there—can ensure the right to vote when local officials are determined to deny it.

In such a case our duty must be clear to all of us. The Constitution says that no person shall be kept from voting because of his race or his color. We have all sworn an oath before God to support and to defend that Constitution. We must now act in obedience to that oath.

Wednesday I will send to Congress a law designed to eliminate illegal barriers to the right to vote. . . .

This bill will strike down restrictions to voting in all elections—Federal, State, and local—which have been used to deny Negroes the right to vote.

This bill will establish a simple, uniform standard which cannot be used, however ingenious the effort, to flout our Constitution. . . .

To those who seek to avoid action by their National Government in their own communities; who want to and who seek to maintain purely local control over elections, the answer is simple:

Open your polling places to all your people.

Allow men and women to register and vote whatever the color of their skin.

Extend the rights of citizenship to every citizen of this land. . . .

But even if we pass this bill, the battle will not be over. What happened in Selma is part of a far larger movement which reaches into every section and State of America. It is the effort of American Negroes to secure for themselves the full blessings of American life.

Their cause must be our cause too. Because it is not just Negroes, but really it is all of us, who must overcome the crippling legacy of bigotry and injustice.

And we shall overcome. . . .

Chapter 30

"THE GREAT
SILENT MAJORITY"

RICHARD NIXON'S
SPEECH ON VIETNAM,
NOVEMBER 3, 1969

☞ Richard Nixon won the presidency in 1968, one of the most tumultuous and tragic years in U.S. history. With an unpopular war raging in Vietnam and the nation bitterly divided on an array of social, cultural, and political issues, Nixon promised to bring the nation together. A year after his election, Nixon delivered a televised speech in which he discussed attempts to train America's allies in South Vietnam to do more of the fighting against a communist insurgency—a policy that would become known as "Vietnamization." But the speech's rhetorical high point was Nixon's appeal for support from what he called the "great silent majority" of Americans. Nixon hoped to capitalize on the alienation of Americans who were skeptical of antiwar protesters and other dissenters who were a constant presence in American culture in the 1960s.

Tonight I want to talk to you on a subject of deep concern to all Americans and to many people in all parts of the world—the war in Vietnam.

I believe that one of the reasons for the deep division about Vietnam is that many Americans have lost confidence in what their Government has told them about our policy. The American people cannot and should not be asked to support a policy which involves the overriding issues of war and peace unless they know the truth about that policy. . . .

It has become clear that the obstacle in negotiating an end to the war is not the President of the United States. It is not the South Vietnamese Government.

The obstacle is the other side's absolute refusal to show the least willingness to join us in seeking a just peace. And it will not do so while it is convinced that all it has to do is to wait for our next concession, and our next concession after that one, until it gets everything it wants. . . .

Now let me turn, however, to a more encouraging report on another front.

At the time we launched our search for peace I recognized we might not succeed in bringing an end to the war through negotiation. I, therefore, put into effect another plan to bring peace—a plan which will bring the war to an end regardless of what happens on the negotiating front.

It is in line with a major shift in U.S. foreign policy which I described in my press conference at Guam on July 25. Let me briefly explain what has been described as the Nixon Doctrine—a policy which not only will help end the war in Vietnam, but which is an essential element of our program to prevent future Vietnams. . . .

Before any American troops were committed to Vietnam, a leader of another Asian country expressed this opinion to me when I was traveling in Asia as a private citizen. He said: "When you are trying to assist another nation defend its freedom, U.S. policy should be to help them fight the war but not to fight the war for them."

Well, in accordance with this wise counsel, I laid down in Guam three principles as guidelines for future American policy toward Asia:

First, the United States will keep all of its treaty commitments.

Second, we shall provide a shield if a nuclear power threatens the freedom of a nation allied with us or of a nation whose survival we consider vital to our security.

Third, in cases involving other types of aggression, we shall furnish military and economic assistance when requested in accordance with our treaty commitments. But we shall look to the nation directly threatened to assume the primary responsibility of providing the manpower for its defense. . . .

In the previous administration, we Americanized the war in Vietnam. In this administration, we are Vietnamizing the search for peace.

The policy of the previous administration not only resulted in our assuming the primary responsibility for fighting the war, but even more significantly did not adequately stress the goal of strengthening the South Vietnamese so that they could defend themselves when we left.

The Vietnamization plan was launched following Secretary Laird's visit to Vietnam in March. Under the plan, I ordered first a substantial increase in the training and equipment of South Vietnamese forces. . . .

And now we have begun to see the results of this long overdue change in American policy in Vietnam.

After five years of Americans going into Vietnam, we are finally bringing American men home. By December 15, over 60,000 men will have been withdrawn from South Vietnam—including 20 percent of all of our combat forces.

The South Vietnamese have continued to gain in strength. As a result they have been able to take over combat responsibilities from our American troops....

We have adopted a plan which we have worked out in cooperation with the South Vietnamese for the complete withdrawal of all U.S. combat ground forces, and their replacement by South Vietnamese forces on an orderly scheduled timetable. This withdrawal will be made from strength and not from weakness. As South Vietnamese forces become stronger, the rate of American withdrawal can become greater....

My fellow Americans, I am sure you can recognize from what I have said that we really only have two choices open to us if we want to end this war.

I can order an immediate, precipitate withdrawal of all Americans from Vietnam without regard to the effects of that action.

Or we can persist in our search for a just peace through a negotiated settlement if possible, or through continued implementation of our plan for Vietnamization if necessary—a plan in which we will withdraw all of our forces from Vietnam on a schedule in accordance with our program, as the South Vietnamese become strong enough to defend their own freedom. I have chosen this second course. It is not the easy way. It is the right way....

And so tonight—to you, the great silent majority of my fellow Americans—I ask for your support.

I pledged in my campaign for the Presidency to end the war in a way that we could win the peace. I have initiated a plan of action which will enable me to keep that pledge.

The more support I can have from the American people, the sooner that pledge can be redeemed, for the more divided we are at home, the less likely the enemy is to negotiate at Paris.

Let us be united for peace. Let us also be united against defeat. Because let us understand: North Vietnam cannot defeat or humiliate the United States. Only Americans can do that....

Chapter 31

"I HAVE FINALLY
BEEN INCLUDED"

BARBARA JORDAN'S SPEECH TO THE
HOUSE JUDICIARY COMMITTEE,
JULY 25, 1974

🖎 In the spring of 1974, the House of Representatives took the first steps toward the possible impeachment of President Richard Nixon—the first such proceedings since Andrew Johnson was impeached (but not removed from office) in 1868. Members of the House Judiciary Committee were given the responsibility of judging which charges against the President rose to the level of impeachable offenses. As members prepared to vote on the articles of impeachment, Representative Barbara Jordan of Texas, an African-American woman known for her eloquence and her deliberate speaking style, delivered extemporaneous remarks which offered not only a brilliant exposition of constitutional law, but also acknowledged the historical irony of her situation. The men who wrote the Constitution created no place for a black woman in the new nation's politics. But on this momentous occasion, she was called on to stand in judgment of a President of the United States.

Earlier today, we heard the beginning of the Preamble to the Constitution of the United States: "We, the people." It is a very eloquent beginning. But when that document was completed on the seventeenth of September in 1787, I was not included in that "We, the people." I felt somehow for many years that George Washington and Alexander Hamilton just left me out by mistake. But through the process of amendment, interpretation, and court decision, I have finally been included in "We, the people."

Today I am an inquisitor. . . . My faith in the Constitution is whole; it is complete; it is total. And I am not going to sit here and be an idle spectator to the diminution, the subversion, the destruction, of the Constitution. . . .

It is wrong, I suggest, it is a misreading of the Constitution for any member here to assert that for a member to vote for an article of impeachment means that that member must be convinced that the President should be removed from office. The Constitution doesn't say that. The powers relating to impeachment are an essential check in the hands of the body of the legislature against and upon the encroachments of the executive. The division between the two branches of the legislature, the House and the Senate, assigning to the one the right to accuse and to the other the right to judge, the framers of this Constitution were very astute. They did not make the accusers . . . and the judges the same person.

We know the nature of impeachment. We've been talking about it awhile now. It is chiefly designed for the President and his high ministers to somehow be called into account. It is designed to "bridle" the executive if he engages in excesses. . . . The framers confided in the Congress the power if need be, to remove the President in order to strike a delicate balance between a President swollen with power and grown tyrannical, and preservation of the independence of the executive.

The nature of impeachment: a narrowly channeled exception to the separation-of-powers maxim. The Federal Convention of 1787 said that. It limited impeachment to high crimes and misdemeanors and discounted and opposed the term "maladministration." "It is to be used only for great misdemeanors," so it was said in the North Carolina ratification convention. . . .

The drawing of political lines goes to the motivation behind impeachment; but impeachment must proceed within the confines of the constitutional term "high crime[s] and misdemeanors." Of the impeachment process, it was Woodrow Wilson who said that "Nothing short of the grossest offenses against the plain law of the land will suffice to give them speed and effectiveness. Indignation so great as to overgrow party interest may secure a conviction; but nothing else can."

Common sense would be revolted if we engaged upon this process for petty reasons. Congress has a lot to do: appropriations, tax reform, health insurance, campaign finance reform, housing, environmental protection, energy sufficiency, mass transportation. Pettiness cannot be allowed to stand in the face of such overwhelming problems. So today we are not being petty. We are trying to be big, because the task we have before us is a big one. . . .

We were further cautioned today that perhaps these proceedings ought to be delayed because certainly there would be new evidence forthcoming from the

Chapter 32

"I HAVE NEVER BEEN
A QUITTER"

RICHARD NIXON'S
RESIGNATION SPEECH,
AUGUST 8, 1974

☞ The Watergate scandal doomed Richard Nixon's presidency in the summer of 1974. Nixon had tried to hold on to office as the scandal mushroomed, insisting that he would fight to the end to clear his name and save his presidency. But when the U.S. Supreme Court ruled unanimously in late July that Nixon had to surrender a series of tape-recorded conversations, the end was inevitable. The recordings showed that Nixon was involved in covering up an attempted break-in at Democratic headquarters in the Watergate Hotel. Support for the President evaporated, leading to this historic speech.

Throughout the long and difficult period of Watergate, I have felt it was my duty to persevere; to make every possible effort to complete the term of office to which you elected me.

In the past few days, however, it has become evident to me that I no longer have a strong enough political base in the Congress to justify continuing that effort.

As long as there was such a base, I felt strongly that it was necessary to see the constitutional process through to its conclusion; that to do otherwise would be unfaithful to the spirit of that deliberately difficult process, and a dangerously destabilizing precedent for the future.

But with the disappearance of that base, I now believe that the constitutional purpose has been served. And there is no longer a need for the process to be prolonged.

I would have preferred to carry through to the finish whatever the personal agony it would have involved, and my family unanimously urged me to do so. But the interests of the nation must always come before any personal considerations. From the discussions I have had with Congressional and other leaders I have concluded that because of the Watergate matter I might not have the support of the Congress that I would consider necessary to back the very difficult decisions and carry out the duties of this office in the way the interests of the nation will require.

I have never been a quitter.

To leave office before my term is completed is opposed to every instinct in my body. But as President I must put the interests of America first.

America needs a full-time President and a full-time Congress, particularly at this time with problems we face at home and abroad.

To continue to fight through the months ahead for my personal vindication would almost totally absorb the time and attention of both the President and the Congress in a period when our entire focus should be on the great issues of peace abroad and prosperity without inflation at home.

Therefore, I shall resign the Presidency effective at noon tomorrow.

Vice President Ford will be sworn in as President at that hour in this office. As I recall the high hopes for America with which we began this second term, I feel a great sadness that I will not be here in this office working on your behalf to achieve those hopes in the next two and a half years.

But in turning over direction of the Government to Vice President Ford I know, as I told the nation when I nominated him for that office 10 months ago, that the leadership of America will be in good hands.

In passing this office to the Vice President I also do so with the profound sense of the weight of responsibility that will fall on his shoulders tomorrow, and therefore of the understanding, the patience, the cooperation he will need from all Americans.

As he assumes that responsibility he will deserve the help and the support of all of us. As we look to the future, the first essential is to begin healing the wounds of this nation. To put the bitterness and divisions of the recent past behind us and to rediscover those shared ideals that lie at the heart of our strength and unity as a great and as a free people.

By taking this action, I hope that I will have hastened the start of that process of healing which is so desperately needed in America.

I regret deeply any injuries that may have been done in the course of the events that led to this decision. I would say only that if some of my judgments were wrong—and some were wrong—they were made in what I believed at the time to be the best interests of the nation.

To those who have stood with me during these past difficult months, to my family, my friends, the many others who joined in supporting my cause because they believed it was right, I will be eternally grateful for your support.

And to those who have not felt able to give me your support, let me say I leave with no bitterness toward those who have opposed me, because all of us in the final analysis have been concerned with the good of the country however our judgments might differ.

So let us all now join together in firming that common commitment and in helping our new President succeed for the benefit of all Americans. . . .

Chapter 33
"A CRISIS OF CONFIDENCE"

JIMMY CARTER'S SPEECH
TO THE NATION,
JULY 15, 1979

☞ Inflation, a stagnant economy, and high oil prices bedeviled the administration of President Jimmy Carter, elected in 1976 after having served a single two-year term as Governor of Georgia. In an attempt to rejuvenate his administration in the summer of 1979, Carter summoned public policy experts and others to the presidential retreat in Camp David, Maryland, to discuss a new course for the country. After ten days of talks, the President emerged to give this speech to the nation. Though it was widely derided as "the malaise speech," Carter never actually uttered that word, malaise. But he did state that the nation was discouraged, an assertion that did little to inspire new confidence in his administration. The speech, however, does speak to a bleak time in U.S. history and culture.

During the past three years I've spoken to you on many occasions about national concerns, the energy crisis, reorganizing the government, our nation's economy, and issues of war and especially peace. But over those years the subjects of the speeches, the talks, and the press conferences have become increasingly narrow, focused more and more on what the isolated world of Washington thinks is important. Gradually, you've heard more and more about what the government thinks or what the government should be doing and less and less about our nation's hopes, our dreams, and our vision of the future.

Ten days ago I had planned to speak to you again about a very important subject—energy. For the fifth time I would have described the urgency of the problem and laid out a series of legislative recommendations to the Congress. But as I was preparing to speak, I began to ask myself the same question that I now know has been troubling many of you. Why have we not been able to get together as a nation to resolve our serious energy problem?

It's clear that the true problems of our nation are much deeper—deeper than gasoline lines or energy shortages, deeper even than inflation or recession. And I realize more than ever that as President I need your help. . . .

These 10 days confirmed my belief in the decency and the strength and the wisdom of the American people, but it also bore out some of my long-standing concerns about our Nation's underlying problems. . . .

So, I want to speak to you first tonight about a subject even more serious than energy or inflation. I want to talk to you right now about a fundamental threat to American democracy. . . .

The threat is nearly invisible in ordinary ways. It is a crisis of confidence. It is a crisis that strikes at the very heart and soul and spirit of our national will. We can see this crisis in the growing doubt about the meaning of our own lives and in the loss of a unity of purpose for our Nation.

The erosion of our confidence in the future is threatening to destroy the social and the political fabric of America.

The confidence that we have always had as a people is not simply some romantic dream or a proverb in a dusty book that we read just on the Fourth of July.

It is the idea which founded our Nation and has guided our development as a people. Confidence in the future has supported everything else—public institutions and private enterprise, our own families, and the very Constitution of the United States. Confidence has defined our course and has served as a link between generations. We've always believed in something called progress. We've always had a faith that the days of our children would be better than our own.

Our people are losing that faith, not only in government itself but in the ability as citizens to serve as the ultimate rulers and shapers of our democracy. . . . The symptoms of this crisis of the American spirit are all around us. For the first time in the history of our country a majority of our people believe that the next five years will be worse than the past five years. Two-thirds of our people do not even vote. The productivity of American workers is actually dropping, and the willingness of Americans to save for the future has fallen below that of all other people in the Western world. . . .

These changes did not happen overnight. They've come upon us gradually over the last generation, years that were filled with shocks and tragedy. . . .

What can we do?

First of all, we must face the truth, and then we can change our course. We simply must have faith in each other, faith in our ability to govern ourselves, and faith in the future of this Nation. Restoring that faith and that confidence to America is now the most important task we face. It is a true challenge of this generation of Americans. . . .

I do not promise a quick way out of our nation's problems, when the truth is that the only way out is an all-out effort. What I do promise you is that I will lead our fight, and I will enforce fairness in our struggle, and I will ensure honesty. And above all, I will act. We can manage the short-term shortages more effectively and we will, but there are no short-term solutions to our long-range problems. There is simply no way to avoid sacrifice. . . .

Little by little we can and we must rebuild our confidence. We can spend until we empty our treasuries, and we may summon all the wonders of science. But we can succeed only if we tap our greatest resources— America's people, America's values, and America's confidence. . . .

Chapter 34

"GOVERNMENT IS THE PROBLEM"

**RONALD REAGAN'S
FIRST INAUGURAL ADDRESS,
JANUARY 20, 1981**

☞ After a decade of political, social, and economic turmoil, Ronald Reagan, a movie star turned politician, was elected President in 1980. His rise to the nation's highest office represented the triumph of a rejuvenated conservative movement which rejected the federal government's expanded presence in the nation's economic life. Reagan's triumph also represented a political coming of age for Sunbelt states, especially California, Texas, and Florida, which replaced the Northeast as the nation's most potent regional bloc. In his inaugural speech as President, Reagan made it clear that he wished to chart a very different course for the nation. He emphasized individual effort, self-reliance, and a pioneering spirit, arguing that prosperity would return only when government got out of the way of the American people.

These United States are confronted with an economic affliction of great proportions. We suffer from the longest and one of the worst sustained inflations in our national history. It distorts our economic decisions, penalizes thrift, and crushes the struggling young and the fixed-income elderly alike. It threatens to shatter the lives of millions of our people.

Idle industries have cast workers into unemployment, human misery, and personal indignity. Those who do work are denied a fair return for their labor by a tax system which penalizes successful achievement and keeps us from maintaining full productivity.

But great as our tax burden is, it has not kept pace with public spending. For decades we have piled deficit upon deficit, mortgaging our future and our children's future for the temporary convenience of the present. To continue this long trend is to guarantee tremendous social, cultural, political, and economic upheavals.

You and I, as individuals, can, by borrowing, live beyond our means, but for only a limited period of time. Why, then, should we think that collectively, as a nation, we're not bound by that same limitation? We must act today in order to preserve tomorrow. And let there be no misunderstanding: We are going to begin to act, beginning today.

The economic ills we suffer have come upon us over several decades. They will not go away in days, weeks, or months, but they will go away. They will go away because we as Americans have the capacity now, as we've had in the past, to do whatever needs to be done to preserve this last and greatest bastion of freedom.

In this present crisis, government is not the solution to our problem; government is the problem. From time to time we've been tempted to believe that society has become too complex to be managed by self-rule, that government by an elite group is superior to government for, by, and of the people. Well, if no one among us is capable of governing himself, then who among us has the capacity to govern someone else? All of us together, in and out of government, must bear the burden. The solutions we seek must be equitable, with no one group singled out to pay a higher price. . . .

It is my intention to curb the size and influence of the Federal establishment and to demand recognition of the distinction between the powers granted to the Federal Government and those reserved to the States or to the people. All of us need to be reminded that the Federal Government did not create the States; the States created the Federal Government. . . .

If we look to the answer as to why for so many years we achieved so much, prospered as no other people on Earth, it was because here in this land we unleashed the energy and individual genius of man to a greater extent than has ever been done before. Freedom and the dignity of the individual have been more available and assured here than in any other place on Earth. The price for this freedom at times has been high, but we have never been unwilling to pay that price.

It is no coincidence that our present troubles parallel and are proportionate to the intervention and intrusion in our lives that result from unnecessary and excessive growth of government. It is time for us to realize that we're too great a nation to limit ourselves to small dreams. We're not, as some would have us believe, doomed to an inevitable decline. I do not believe in a fate that will fall on us no matter what we do. I do believe in a fate that will fall on us if we do nothing. So, with all the creative energy at our command, let us begin an era of national renewal. Let us renew our determination, our courage, and our strength. And let us renew our faith and our hope.

We have every right to dream heroic dreams. Those who say that we're in a time when there are not heroes, they just don't know where to look. You can see heroes every day going in and out of factory gates. Others, a handful in number, produce enough food to feed all of us and then the world beyond. You meet heroes across a counter, and they're on both sides of that counter. There are entrepreneurs with faith in themselves and faith in an idea who create new jobs, new wealth and opportunity. They're individuals and families whose taxes support the government and whose voluntary gifts support church, charity, culture, art, and education. Their patriotism is quiet, but deep. Their values sustain our national life. . . .

This is the first time in our history that this ceremony has been held, as you've been told, on this West Front of the Capitol. Standing here, one faces a magnificent vista, opening up on this city's special beauty and history. At the end of this open mall are those shrines to the giants on whose shoulders we stand.

Directly in front of me, the monument to a monumental man, George Washington, father of our country. A man of humility who came to greatness reluctantly. He led America out of revolutionary victory into infant nationhood. Off to one side, the stately memorial to Thomas Jefferson. The Declaration of Independence flames with his eloquence. And then, beyond the Reflecting Pool, the dignified columns of the Lincoln Memorial. Whoever would understand in his heart the meaning of America will find it in the life of Abraham Lincoln.

Beyond those monuments to heroism is the Potomac River, and on the far shore the sloping hills of Arlington National Cemetery, with its row upon row of simple white markers bearing crosses or Stars of David. They add up to only a tiny fraction of the price that has been paid for our freedom.

Each one of those markers is a monument to the kind of hero I spoke of earlier. Their lives ended in places called Belleau Wood, the Argonne, Omaha Beach, Salerno, and halfway around the world on Guadalcanal, Tarawa, Pork Chop Hill, the Chosin Reservoir, and in a hundred rice paddies and jungles of a place called Vietnam.

Under one such marker lies a young man, Martin Treptow, who left his job in a small town barbershop in 1917 to go to France with the famed Rainbow Division. There, on the western front, he was killed trying to carry a message between battalions under heavy artillery fire.

We're told that on his body was found a diary. On the flyleaf under the heading, "My Pledge," he had written these words: "America must win this war. Therefore I will work, I will save, I will sacrifice, I will endure, I will fight cheerfully and do my utmost, as if the issue of the whole struggle depended on me alone."

The crisis we are facing today does not require of us the kind of sacrifice that Martin Treptow and so many thousands of others were called upon to make. It does require, however, our best effort and our willingness to believe in ourselves and to believe in our capacity to perform great deeds, to believe that together with God's help we can and will resolve the problems which now confront us.

And after all, why shouldn't we believe that? We are Americans.

Chapter 35

"THE AGGRESSIVE IMPULSES OF AN EVIL EMPIRE"

**RONALD REAGAN'S SPEECH TO
THE NATIONAL ASSOCIATION
OF EVANGELICALS,
MARCH 8, 1983**

"Nuclear freeze" was a popular rallying cry in the United States and around the world in early 1983, as the Reagan administration prepared to introduce a new generation of nuclear missiles in Europe. Critics, including many in Congress, demanded that both the United States and the Soviet Union freeze the deployment of new nuclear weapons. President Reagan rejected the freeze movement, arguing that a freeze would bar the United States from countering a Soviet buildup in eastern Europe. Reagan made his case at a meeting of evangelical ministers in Florida. The speech contained an instantly famous phrase which encapsulated Reagan's view of the Soviet Union and communism.

During my first press conference as president, in answer to a direct question, I pointed out that, as good Marxist-Leninists, the Soviet leaders have openly and publicly declared that the only morality they recognize is that which will further their cause, which is world revolution. I think I should point out I was only quoting Lenin, their guiding spirit, who said in 1920 that they repudiate all morality that proceeds from supernatural ideas—that's their name for religion—or ideas that are outside class conceptions. Morality is entirely subordinate to the interests of class war. And everything is moral that is necessary for the annihilation of the old, exploiting social order and for uniting the proletariat.

Well, I think the refusal of many influential people to accept this elementary fact of Soviet doctrine illustrates a historical reluctance to see totalitarian powers for what they are. We saw this phenomenon in the 1930s. We see it too often today.

This doesn't mean we should isolate ourselves and refuse to seek an understanding with them. I intend to do everything I can to persuade them of our peaceful intent, to remind them that it was the West that refused to use its nuclear monopoly in the '40s and '50s for territorial gain and which now proposes a 50 percent cut in strategic ballistic missiles and the elimination of an entire class of land-based, intermediate-range nuclear missiles.

At the same time, however, they must be made to understand we will never compromise our principles and standards. We will never give away our freedom. We will never abandon our belief in God. And we will never stop searching for a genuine peace. But we can assure none of these things America stands for through the so-called nuclear freeze solutions proposed by some.

The truth is that a freeze now would be a very dangerous fraud, for that is merely the illusion of peace. The reality is that we must find peace through strength.

I would agree to a freeze if only we could freeze the Soviets' global desires. A freeze at current levels of weapons would remove any incentive for the Soviets to negotiate seriously in Geneva and virtually end our chances to achieve the major arms reductions which we have proposed. Instead, they would achieve their objectives through the freeze.

A freeze would reward the Soviet Union for its enormous and unparalleled military buildup. It would prevent the essential and long overdue modernization of United States and allied defenses and would leave our aging forces increasingly vulnerable. And an honest freeze would require extensive prior negotiations on the systems and numbers to be limited and on the measures to ensure effective verification and compliance. And the kind of a freeze that has been suggested would be virtually impossible to verify. Such a major effort would divert us completely from our current negotiations on achieving substantial reductions. . . .

Yes, let us pray for the salvation of all of those who live in that totalitarian darkness. Pray they will discover the joy of knowing God. But until they do, let us be aware that while they preach the supremacy of the State, declare its omnipotence over individual man, and predict its eventual domination of all peoples on the earth, they are the focus of evil in the modern world.

It was C. S. Lewis who, in his unforgettable *Screwtape Letters*, wrote: "The greatest evil is not done now in those sordid 'dens of crime' that Dickens loved to paint. It is not even done in concentration camps and labor camps. In those we see its final result. But it is conceived and ordered; moved, seconded, carried and minuted in clear, carpeted, warmed, and well-lighted offices, by quiet men with white collars and cut fingernails and smooth-shaven cheeks who do not need to raise their voice."

Well, because these quiet men do not raise their voices, because they sometimes speak in soothing tones of brotherhood and peace, because, like other dictators before them, they're always making "their final territorial demand," some would have us accept them at their word and accommodate ourselves to their aggressive impulses. But if history teaches anything, it teaches that simpleminded appeasement or wishful thinking about our adversaries is folly. It means the betrayal of our past, the squandering of our freedom.

So, I urge you to speak out against those who would place the United States in a position of military and moral inferiority. . . . So, in your discussions of the nuclear freeze proposals, I urge you to beware the temptation of pride—the temptation of blithely declaring yourselves above it all and label both sides equally at fault, to ignore the facts of history and the aggressive impulses of an evil empire, to simply call the arms race a giant misunderstanding and thereby remove yourself from the struggle between right and wrong and good and evil.

I ask you to resist the attempts of those who would have you withhold your support for our efforts, this administration's efforts, to keep America strong and free, while we negotiate real and verifiable reductions in the world's nuclear arsenals and one day, with God's help, their total elimination.

While America's military strength is important, let me add here that I've always maintained that the struggle now going on for the world will never be decided by bombs or rockets, by armies or military might. The real crisis we face today is a spiritual one; at root, it is a test of moral will and faith. . . .

I believe that communism is another sad, bizarre chapter in human history whose last pages even now are being written. I believe this because the source of our strength in the quest for human freedom is not material, but spiritual. And because it knows no limitation, it must terrify and ultimately triumph over those who would enslave their fellow man. For in the words of Isaiah: "He giveth power to the faint; and to them that have no might He increases strength. But they that wait upon the Lord shall renew their strength; they shall mount up with wings as eagles; they shall run, and not be weary."

Yes, change your world. One of our Founding Fathers, Thomas Paine, said, "We have it within our power to begin the world over again." We can do it, doing together what no one church could do by itself.

▪▐▐▌▌▐▐▌▌▐▐▌▌▐▐▌▌▐▐▌▌▐▐▌▌▐▐▌▌▐▐ ▪

Chapter 36

"TEAR DOWN
THIS WALL"

▪▐▐▌▌▐▐▌▌▐▐▌▌▐▐▌▌▐▐▌▌▐▐▌▌▐▐▌▌▐▐ ▪

**PRESIDENT REAGAN AT THE
BRANDENBURG GATE, BERLIN,
JUNE 12, 1987**

Like John Kennedy before him, Ronald Reagan found the Berlin Wall to be a perfect symbol of divisions between the liberal democracies of the West and the communist regimes of eastern Europe and elsewhere. Reagan followed in Kennedy's footsteps by delivering an impassioned speech in West Berlin, the lonely outpost of the Western allies deep in the heart of East Germany. Reagan displayed his country's new confidence and self-assurance as he did more than simply condemn those who built and maintained the wall. He challenged the Soviet leader, Mikhail Gorbachev, to tear it down. At the time, Reagan's challenge seemed radical and provocative. Yet the wall came down two years later.

Behind me stands a wall that encircles the free sectors of this city, part of a vast system of barriers that divides the entire continent of Europe. From the Baltic, south, those barriers cut across Germany in a gash of barbed wire, concrete, dog runs, and guardtowers. Farther south, there may be no visible, no obvious wall.

But there remain armed guards and checkpoints all the same—still a restriction on the right to travel, still an instrument to impose upon ordinary men and women the will of a totalitarian state. Yet it is here in Berlin where the wall emerges most clearly; here, cutting across your city, where the news photo and the television screen have imprinted this brutal division of a continent upon the mind of the world. Standing before the Brandenburg Gate, every man is a German, separated from his fellow men. Every man is a Berliner, forced to look upon a scar. . . .

In the 1950s, Khrushchev predicted: "We will bury you." But in the West today, we see a free world that has achieved a level of prosperity and well-being unprecedented in all human history. In the Communist world, we see failure, technological backwardness, declining standards of health, even want of the most basic kind—too little food. Even today, the Soviet Union still cannot feed itself. After these four decades, then, there stands before the entire world one great and inescapable conclusion: Freedom leads to prosperity. Freedom replaces the ancient hatreds among the nations with comity and peace. Freedom is the victor.

And now the Soviets themselves may, in a limited way, be coming to understand the importance of freedom. We hear much from Moscow about a new policy of reform and openness. Some political prisoners have been released. Certain foreign news broadcasts are no longer being jammed. Some economic enterprises have been permitted to operate with greater freedom from state control. Are these the beginnings of profound changes in the Soviet state? Or are they token gestures, intended to raise false hopes in the West, or to strengthen the Soviet system without changing it? We welcome change and openness; for we believe that freedom and security go together, that the advance of human liberty can only strengthen the cause of world peace.

There is one sign the Soviets can make that would be unmistakable, that would advance dramatically the cause of freedom and peace. General Secretary Gorbachev, if you seek peace, if you seek prosperity for the Soviet Union and Eastern Europe, if you seek liberalization: Come here to this gate! Mr. Gorbachev, open this gate! Mr. Gorbachev, tear down this wall! . . .

In these four decades, as I have said, you Berliners have built a great city. You've done so in spite of threats—the Soviet attempts to impose the East-mark, the blockade. Today the city thrives in spite of the challenges implicit in the very presence of this wall. What keeps you here? Certainly there's a great deal to be said for your fortitude, for your defiant courage. But I believe there's something deeper, something that involves Berlin's whole look and feel and way of life—not mere sentiment. No one could live long in Berlin without being completely disabused of illusions. Something instead, that has seen the difficulties of life in Berlin but chose to accept them, that continues to build this good and proud city in contrast to a surrounding totalitarian presence that refuses to release human energies or aspirations. Something that speaks with a powerful voice of affirmation, that says yes to this city, yes to the future, yes to freedom. In a word, I would submit that what keeps you in Berlin is love—love both profound and abiding. . . .

As I looked out a moment ago from the Reichstag,

that embodiment of German unity, I noticed words crudely spray-painted upon the wall, perhaps by a young Berliner, "This wall will fall. Beliefs become reality." Yes, across Europe, this wall will fall. For it cannot withstand faith; it cannot withstand truth. The wall cannot withstand freedom.

And I would like, before I close, to say one word. I have read, and I have been questioned since I've been here about certain demonstrations against my coming. And I would like to say just one thing, and to those who demonstrate so. I wonder if they have ever asked themselves that if they should have the kind of government they apparently seek, no one would ever be able to do what they're doing again.

Chapter 37

"MAKE OUR PEOPLE
WHOLE AGAIN"

PRESIDENT BILL CLINTON PLEADS
FOR DOMESTIC PEACE IN MEMPHIS,
NOVEMBER 13, 1993

🖝 The introduction of a new, cheap, and highly addictive drug, crack cocaine, brought havoc to many impoverished and long-suffering communities in the early 1990s. Cities like New York saw murder rates reach record levels—most of the victims were poor and black or brown. Newly elected President Bill Clinton went to Memphis, Tennessee, to deliver an impassioned speech about crime and its victims from the very pulpit where Martin Luther King, Jr., preached his final sermon in 1968. Clinton used the occasion to argue that government, families, and individuals all had responsibilities to combat the violence that took a fearsome toll in many American communities.

The other day I was in California at a town meeting, and a handsome young man stood up and said, "Mr. President, my brother and I, we don't belong to gangs. We don't have guns. We don't do drugs. We want to go to school. We want to be professionals. We want to work hard. We want to do well. We want to have families. And we changed our school because the school we were in was so dangerous. So when we showed up to the new school to register, my brother and I were standing in line and somebody ran into the school and started shooting a gun. My brother was shot down standing right in front of me at the safer school."

The freedom to do that kind of thing is not what Martin Luther King lived and died for, not what people gathered in this hallowed church for the night before he was assassinated in April of 1968. If you had told anybody who was here in that church on that night that we would abuse our freedom in that way, they would have found it hard to believe. And I tell you, it is our moral duty to turn it around. . . .

And there is something for each of us to do. There are changes we each make from the outside in; that's the job of the President, the Congress, and the Governors and the mayors and the social service agencies. And then there's some changes we're going to have to make from the inside out, or the others won't matter. . . . Sometimes there are no answers from the outside in; sometimes all the answers have to come from the values and the stirrings and the voices that speak to us from within. . . .

The famous African-American sociologist William Julius Wilson has written a stunning book called "The Truly Disadvantaged" in which he chronicles in breathtaking terms how the inner cities of our country have crumbled as work has disappeared. And we must find a way, through public and private sources, to enhance the attractiveness of the American people who live there to get investment there. We cannot, I submit to you, repair the American community and restore the

American family until we provide the structure, the values, the discipline, and the reward that work gives.

I read a wonderful speech the other day given at Howard University in a lecture series funded by Bill and Camille Cosby, in which the speaker said, "I grew up in Anacostia years ago. Even then it was all black, and it was a very poor neighborhood. But you know, when I was a child in Anacostia, a 100 percent African-American neighborhood, a very poor neighborhood, we had a crime rate that was lower than the average of the crime rate of our city. Why? Because we had coherent families. We had coherent communities. . . . We were whole." And I say to you, we have to make our people whole again.

This church has stood for that. Why do you think you have five million members in this country? Because people know you are filled with the spirit of God to do the right thing in this life by them. So I say to you, we have to make a partnership, all the Government agencies, all the business folks; but where there are no families, where there is no order, where there is no hope, where we are reducing the size of our armed services because we have won the cold war, who will be there to give structure, discipline, and love to these children? You must do that. And we must help you. Scripture says, you are the salt of the Earth and the light of the world, that if your light shines before men they will give glow to the Father in heaven. That is what we must do. . . .

And so I say to you today, my fellow Americans, you gave me this job, and we're making progress on the things you hired me to do. But unless we deal with the ravages of crime and drugs and violence and unless we recognize that it's due to the breakdown of the family, the community, and the disappearance of jobs, and unless we say some of this cannot be done by Government, because we have to reach deep inside to the values, the spirit, the soul, and the truth of human nature, none of the other things we seek to do will ever take us where we need to go.

So in this pulpit, on this day, let me ask all of you in your heart to say: We will honor the life and the work of Martin Luther King. We will honor the meaning of our church. We will, somehow, by God's grace, we will turn this around. We will give these children a future. We will take away their guns and give them books. We will take away their despair and give them hope. We will rebuild the families and the neighborhoods and the communities. We won't make all the work that has gone on here benefit just a few. We will do it together by the grace of God.

Chapter 38

"IF WOMEN ARE HEALTHY AND EDUCATED"

HILLARY CLINTON DEFINES WOMEN'S RIGHTS AS HUMAN RIGHTS, SEPTEMBER 5, 1995

🖎 Hillary Clinton was the nation's most outspoken First Lady since Eleanor Roosevelt. In 1995, she led an American delegation to China for a United Nations conference on women's rights. Her presence and her record as an advocate for women's rights elevated the conference's visibility and attracted new attention to the cause of women's rights throughout the world. In this speech there are echoes of President Kennedy's speech at the Berlin Wall. "There are some who question the reason for this conference," Mrs. Clinton said. "Let them listen to the voices of women in their homes." The First Lady and future Secretary of State challenged all societies to provide women with health care, education, and support.

By gathering in Beijing, we are focusing world attention on issues that matter most in our lives—the lives of women and their families: access to education, health care, jobs and credit, the chance to enjoy basic legal and human rights and to participate fully in the political life of our countries.

There are some who question the reason for this conference. Let them listen to the voices of women in their homes, neighborhoods, and workplaces. There are some who wonder whether the lives of women and girls matter to economic and political progress around the globe. Let them look at the women gathered here and at Huairou—the homemakers and nurses, the teachers and lawyers, the policymakers and women who run their own businesses. It is conferences like this that compel governments and peoples everywhere to listen, look, and face the world's most pressing problems. Wasn't it, after all, after the women's conference in Nairobi ten years ago that the world focused for the first time on the crisis of domestic violence? . . .

What we are learning around the world is that if women are healthy and educated, their families will flourish. If women are free from violence, their families will flourish. If women have a chance to work and earn as full and equal partners in society, their families will flourish. And when families flourish, communities and nations do as well. That is why every woman, every man, every child, every family, and every nation on this planet does have a stake in the discussion that takes place here. . . .

The great challenge of this conference is to give voice to women everywhere whose experiences go unnoticed, whose words go unheard. Women comprise more than half the world's population, 70 percent of the world's poor, and two-thirds of those who are not taught to read and write. We are the primary caretakers for most of the world's children and elderly. Yet much of the work we do is not valued—not by economists, not by historians, not by popular culture, not by government leaders.

At this very moment, as we sit here, women around the world are giving birth, raising children, cooking meals, washing clothes, cleaning houses, planting crops, working on assembly lines, running companies, and running countries. Women also are dying from diseases that should have been prevented or treated. They are watching their children succumb to malnutrition caused by poverty and economic deprivation. They are being denied the right to go to school by their own fathers and brothers. They are being forced into prostitution, and they are being barred from the bank lending offices and banned from the ballot box.

Those of us who have the opportunity to be here have the responsibility to speak for those who could not. As an American, I want to speak for those women in my own country, women who are raising children on the minimum wage, women who can't afford health care or child care, women whose lives are threatened by violence, including violence in their own homes. . . .

We need to understand there is no one formula for how women should lead our lives. That is why we must respect the choices that each woman makes for herself and her family. Every woman deserves the chance to realize her own God-given potential. But we must recognize that women will never gain full dignity until their human rights are respected and protected.

Our goals for this conference, to strengthen families and societies by empowering women to take greater control over their own destinies, cannot be fully achieved unless all governments—here and around the

world—accept their responsibility to protect and promote internationally recognized human rights. The international community has long acknowledged and
recently reaffirmed at Vienna that both women and
men are entitled to a range of protections and personal
freedoms, from the right of personal security to the
right to determine freely the number and spacing of
the children they bear. No one should be forced to remain silent for fear of religious or political persecution,
arrest, abuse, or torture.

Tragically, women are most often the ones whose
human rights are violated. Even now, in the late 20th
century, the rape of women continues to be used as an
instrument of armed conflict. Women and children
make up a large majority of the world's refugees. And
when women are excluded from the political process,
they become even more vulnerable to abuse. I believe
that now, on the eve of a new millennium, it is time to
break the silence. It is time for us to say here in Beijing,
and for the world to hear, that it is no longer acceptable
to discuss women's rights as separate from human
rights. . . .

It is a violation of human rights when babies are
denied food, or drowned, or suffocated, or their spines
broken, simply because they are born girls.

It is a violation of human rights when women and
girls are sold into the slavery of prostitution for human
greed—and the kinds of reasons that are used to justify
this practice should no longer be tolerated.

It is a violation of human rights when women are
doused with gasoline, set on fire, and burned to death
because their marriage dowries are deemed too small.

It is a violation of human rights when individual

women are raped in their own communities and when thousands of women are subjected to rape as a tactic or prize of war.

It is a violation of human rights when a leading cause of death worldwide among women ages 14 to 44 is the violence they are subjected to in their own homes by their own relatives.

It is a violation of human rights when young girls are brutalized by the painful and degrading practice of genital mutilation.

It is a violation of human rights when women are denied the right to plan their own families, and that includes being forced to have abortions or being sterilized against their will.

If there is one message that echoes forth from this conference, let it be that human rights are women's rights and women's rights are human rights once and for all. Let us not forget that among those rights are the right to speak freely—and the right to be heard.

Women must enjoy the rights to participate fully in the social and political lives of their countries, if we want freedom and democracy to thrive and endure. It is indefensible that many women in nongovernmental organizations who wished to participate in this conference have not been able to attend—or have been prohibited from fully taking part.

Let me be clear. Freedom means the right of people to assemble, organize, and debate openly. It means respecting the views of those who may disagree with the views of their governments. It means not taking citizens away from their loved ones and jailing them, mistreating them, or denying them their freedom or dignity because of the peaceful expression of their ideas and opinions. . . .

Now it is the time to act on behalf of women everywhere. If we take bold steps to better the lives of women, we will be taking bold steps to better the lives of children and families too. Families rely on mothers and wives for emotional support and care. Families rely on women for labor in the home. And increasingly, everywhere, families rely on women for income needed to raise healthy children and care for other relatives.

As long as discrimination and inequities remain so commonplace everywhere in the world, as long as girls and women are valued less, fed less, fed last, overworked, underpaid, not schooled, subjected to violence in and outside their homes—the potential of the human family to create a peaceful, prosperous world will not be realized. . . .

The time is now. We must move beyond rhetoric. We must move beyond recognition of problems to working together, to have the common efforts to build that common ground we hope to see.

Chapter 39

"WE SHALL NOT FALTER"

**GEORGE W. BUSH'S ADDRESS AFTER
THE 9/11 ATTACKS,
SEPTEMBER 20, 2001**

Terrorists using hijacked jetliners destroyed the World Trade Center in Manhattan and damaged a portion of the Pentagon on September 11, 2001. The attack killed nearly three thousand civilians, most of them in the Trade Center's two towers. Most Americans had heard of neither the organization which planned the assault, al Qaeda, nor its leader, Osama bin Laden. President George W. Bush addressed the nation from Capitol Hill on September 20, vowing to avenge the attacks and bring the terrorists to justice. He also called on nations that supported terrorism to cease their activities or face certain punishment.

On September the 11th, enemies of freedom committed an act of war against our country. Americans have known wars—but for the past 136 years, they have been wars on foreign soil, except for one Sunday in 1941. Americans have known the casualties of war—but not at the center of a great city on a peaceful morning. Americans have known surprise attacks—but never before on thousands of civilians. All of this was brought upon us in a single day—and night fell on a different world, a world where freedom itself is under attack.

Americans have many questions tonight. Americans are asking: Who attacked our country? The evidence we have gathered all points to a collection of loosely affiliated terrorist organizations known as al Qaeda. They are the same murderers indicted for bombing American embassies in Tanzania and Kenya, and responsible for bombing the USS *Cole*.

Al Qaeda is to terror what the mafia is to crime. But its goal is not making money; its goal is remaking the world—and imposing its radical beliefs on people everywhere.

The terrorists practice a fringe form of Islamic extremism that has been rejected by Muslim scholars and the vast majority of Muslim clerics—a fringe movement that perverts the peaceful teachings of Islam. The terrorists' directive commands them to kill Christians and Jews, to kill all Americans, and make no distinction among military and civilians, including women and children.

This group and its leader—a person named Osama bin Laden—are linked to many other organizations in different countries, including the Egyptian Islamic Jihad and the Islamic Movement of Uzbekistan. There are thousands of these terrorists in more than 60 countries. They are recruited from their own nations and neighborhoods and brought to camps in places like Afghanistan, where they are trained in the tactics of terror. They are sent back to their homes or sent to hide in countries around the world to plot evil and destruction.

The leadership of al Qaeda has great influence in Afghanistan and supports the Taliban regime in controlling most of that country. In Afghanistan, we see al Qaeda's vision for the world. . . .

The United States respects the people of Afghanistan—after all, we are currently its largest source of humanitarian aid—but we condemn the Taliban regime. It is not only repressing its own people, it is threatening people everywhere by sponsoring and sheltering and supplying terrorists. By aiding and abetting murder, the Taliban regime is committing murder.

And tonight, the United States of America makes the following demands on the Taliban: Deliver to United States authorities all the leaders of al Qaeda who hide in your land. Release all foreign nationals, including American citizens, you have unjustly imprisoned. Protect foreign journalists, diplomats and aid workers in your country. Close immediately and permanently every terrorist training camp in Afghanistan, and hand over every terrorist, and every person in their support structure, to appropriate authorities. Give the United States full access to terrorist training camps, so we can make sure they are no longer operating.

These demands are not open to negotiation or discussion. The Taliban must act, and act immediately. They will hand over the terrorists, or they will share in their fate.

I also want to speak tonight directly to Muslims throughout the world. We respect your faith. It's practiced freely by many millions of Americans, and by millions more in countries that America counts as friends. Its teachings are good and peaceful, and those who commit evil in the name of Allah blaspheme the name of Allah. The terrorists are traitors to their own faith, trying, in effect, to hijack Islam itself. The enemy of America is not our many Muslim friends; it is not our many Arab friends. Our enemy is a radical network of terrorists, and every government that supports them.

Our war on terror begins with al Qaeda, but it does not end there. It will not end until every terrorist group of global reach has been found, stopped and defeated.

Americans are asking, why do they hate us? They hate what we see right here in this chamber—a democratically elected government. Their leaders are self-appointed. They hate our freedoms—our freedom of religion, our freedom of speech, our freedom to vote and assemble and disagree with each other.

They want to overthrow existing governments in many Muslim countries, such as Egypt, Saudi Arabia, and Jordan. They want to drive Israel out of the Middle East. They want to drive Christians and Jews out of vast regions of Asia and Africa. . . .

We are not deceived by their pretenses to piety. We have seen their kind before. They are the heirs of all the murderous ideologies of the 20th century. By sacrificing human life to serve their radical visions—by abandoning every value except the will to power—they follow in the path of fascism, and Nazism, and totalitarianism. And they will follow that path all the way, to where it ends: in history's unmarked grave of discarded lies. . . .

Every nation, in every region, now has a decision to make. Either you are with us, or you are with the terrorists. From this day forward, any nation that continues to harbor or support terrorism will be regarded by the United States as a hostile regime. . . .

Great harm has been done to us. We have suffered great loss. And in our grief and anger we have found our mission and our moment. Freedom and fear are at war. The advance of human freedom—the great achievement of our time, and the great hope of every time—now depends on us. Our nation—this generation—will lift a dark threat of violence from our people and our future. We will rally the world to this cause by our efforts, by our courage. We will not tire, we will not falter, and we will not fail.

Chapter 40

"LET US BRAVE ONCE MORE THE ICY CURRENTS"

BARACK OBAMA'S INAUGURAL ADDRESS, JANUARY 20, 2009

Barack Obama took office as President in the midst of what would prove to be the nation's worst economic crisis since the Great Depression. What's more, the United States was fighting two wars overseas, one in Iraq, the other in Afghanistan. The national mood was grim, but the occasion was historic. Obama was the first African American to be elected to the nation's highest office, a milestone which would have seemed unreachable only a few years earlier. The new President focused his attention on the nation's plight, not his achievement, although he did make a passing reference to the reality that his African-born father would not have been served at many lunch counters in midcentury America.

We remain a young nation, but in the words of Scripture, the time has come to set aside childish things. The time has come to reaffirm our enduring spirit, to choose our better history, to carry forward that precious gift, that noble idea, passed on from generation to generation: the God-given promise that all are equal, all are free, and all deserve a chance to pursue their full measure of happiness.

In reaffirming the greatness of our nation, we understand that greatness is never a given. It must be earned. Our journey has never been one of shortcuts or settling for less. It has not been the path for the faint-hearted—for those who prefer leisure over work, or seek only the pleasures of riches and fame. Rather, it has been the risk-takers, the doers, the makers of things—some celebrated but more often men and women obscure in their labor, who have carried us up the long, rugged path towards prosperity and freedom.

For us, they packed up their few worldly possessions and traveled across oceans in search of a new life.

For us, they toiled in sweatshops and settled the West; endured the lash of the whip and plowed the hard earth.

For us, they fought and died, in places like Concord and Gettysburg; Normandy, and Khe Sahn.

Time and again these men and women struggled and sacrificed and worked till their hands were raw so that we might live a better life. They saw America as bigger than the sum of our individual ambitions; greater than all the differences of birth or wealth or faction.

This is the journey we continue today. We remain the most prosperous, powerful nation on Earth. Our workers are no less productive than when this crisis began. Our minds are no less inventive, our goods and services no less needed than they were last week or last month or last year. Our capacity remains undiminished.

But our time of standing pat, of protecting narrow interests and putting off unpleasant decisions—that time has surely passed. Starting today, we must pick ourselves up, dust ourselves off, and begin again the work of remaking America. . . .

Now, there are some who question the scale of our ambitions—who suggest that our system cannot tolerate too many big plans. Their memories are short. For they have forgotten what this country has already done; what free men and women can achieve when imagination is joined to common purpose, and necessity to courage. . . .

As for our common defense, we reject as false the choice between our safety and our ideals. Our Founding Fathers, faced with perils we can scarcely imagine, drafted a charter to assure the rule of law and the rights of man, a charter expanded by the blood of generations. Those ideals still light the world, and we will not give them up for expedience's sake. And so to all other peoples and governments who are watching today, from the grandest capitals to the small village where my father was born: Know that America is a friend of each nation and every man, woman, and child who seeks a future of peace and dignity, and that we are ready to lead once more.

Recall that earlier generations faced down fascism and communism not just with missiles and tanks, but with the sturdy alliances and enduring convictions. They understood that our power alone cannot protect us, nor does it entitle us to do as we please. Instead, they knew that our power grows through its prudent use; our security emanates from the justness of our

cause, the force of our example, the tempering qualities of humility and restraint.

We are the keepers of this legacy. Guided by these
principles once more, we can meet those new threats
that demand even greater effort—even greater cooperation and understanding between nations. We will
begin to responsibly leave Iraq to its people, and forge
a hard-earned peace in Afghanistan. With old friends
and former foes, we will work tirelessly to lessen the
nuclear threat, and roll back the specter of a warming
planet. We will not apologize for our way of life, nor
will we waver in its defense, and for those who seek to
advance their aims by inducing terror and slaughter-
ing innocents, we say to you now that our spirit is
stronger and cannot be broken; you cannot outlast us,
and we will defeat you.

For we know that our patchwork heritage is a
strength, not a weakness. We are a nation of Christians and Muslims, Jews and Hindus—and non-
believers. We are shaped by every language and
culture, drawn from every end of this Earth; and because we have tasted the bitter swill of civil war and
segregation, and emerged from that dark chapter
stronger and more united, we cannot help but believe
that the old hatreds shall someday pass; that the lines
of tribe shall soon dissolve; that as the world grows
smaller, our common humanity shall reveal itself; and
that America must play its role in ushering in a new
era of peace.

To the Muslim world, we seek a new way forward,
based on mutual interest and mutual respect. To those
leaders around the globe who seek to sow conflict, or

blame their society's ills on the West—know that your people will judge you on what you can build, not what you destroy. To those who cling to power through corruption and deceit and the silencing of dissent, know that you are on the wrong side of history, but that we will extend a hand if you are willing to unclench your fist. . . .

Our challenges may be new, the instruments with which we meet them may be new. But those values upon which our success depends—honesty and hard work, courage and fair play, tolerance and curiosity, loyalty and patriotism—these things are old. These things are true. They have been the quiet force of progress throughout our history. What is demanded then is a return to these truths. What is required of us now is a new era of responsibility—a recognition, on the part of every American, that we have duties to ourselves, our nation, and the world, duties that we do not grudgingly accept but rather seize gladly, firm in the knowledge that there is nothing so satisfying to the spirit, so defining of our character, than giving our all to a difficult task.

This is the price and the promise of citizenship.

This is the source of our confidence—the knowledge that God calls on us to shape an uncertain destiny.

This is the meaning of our liberty and our creed—why men and women and children of every race and every faith can join in celebration across this magnificent mall, and why a man whose father less than 60 years ago might not have been served at a local restaurant can now stand before you to take a most sacred oath.

So let us mark this day with remembrance, of who

we are and how far we have traveled. In the year of America's birth, in the coldest of months, a small band of patriots huddled by dying campfires on the shores of an icy river. The capital was abandoned. The enemy was advancing. The snow was stained with blood. At a moment when the outcome of our revolution was most in doubt, the father of our nation ordered these words be read to the people:

"Let it be told to the future world . . . that in the depth of winter, when nothing but hope and virtue could survive . . . that the city and the country, alarmed at one common danger, came forth to meet it."

America, in the face of our common dangers, in this winter of our hardship, let us remember these timeless words. With hope and virtue, let us brave once more the icy currents, and endure what storms may come. Let it be said by our children's children that when we were tested, we refused to let this journey end, that we did not turn back nor did we falter; and with eyes fixed on the horizon and God's grace upon us, we carried forth that great gift of freedom and delivered it safely to future generations.

Cover art for the Penguin Civic Classics series draws from early American ephemera and was initially inspired by Benjamin Franklin's "Join, or Die" political cartoon, a woodcut print of a divided snake first published in the *Pennsylvania Gazette* in 1754 to stress the importance of colonial unity. Reinterpreted in modern graphic style, these evocative images and symbols have continued to provoke and inspire into the present day.

———•◆•———

The text is set primarily in Adobe Caslon, a version of which was used extensively throughout America's colonial period. Indeed, the first printings of the Declaration of Independence and the Constitution were printed in Caslon.